ROUTLEDGE LIBRARY EDITIONS: ISLAM

A SUFI MARTYR

A SUFI MARTYR

The *Apologia* of 'Ain al-Quḍāt al-Hamadhānī

Translated with introduction and notes by

A. J. ARBERRY

Volume 43

Routledge
Taylor & Francis Group
LONDON AND NEW YORK

First published in paperback 2024

First published in 1969
This edition first published in 2008 by
Routledge
4 Park Square, Milton Park, Abingdon, Oxon OX14 4RN

and by Routledge
605 Third Avenue, New York, NY 10158

Routledge is an imprint of the Taylor & Francis Group, an informa business

Publisher's Note
The publisher has gone to great lengths to ensure the quality of this reprint but points out that some imperfections in the original copies may be apparent.

British Library Cataloguing in Publication Data
A catalogue record for this book is available from the British Library

Library of Congress Cataloging in Publication Data
A catalog record for this book has been requested

ISBN: 978-0-415-42600-8 (set)
ISBN: 978-0-415-44258-9 (hbk) (vol xliii)
ISBN: 978-1-03-258743-1 (pbk)
ISBN: 978-1-315-88818-7 (ebk)

DOI: 10.4324/9781315888187

A Sufi Martyr

The *Apologia* of 'Ain al-Quḍāt al-Hamadhānī

Translated
with Introduction and Notes
by

A. J. ARBERRY

London

GEORGE ALLEN AND UNWIN LTD

RUSKIN HOUSE · MUSEUM STREET

FIRST PUBLISHED IN 1969

SBN 04 297020 2

PRINTED IN GREAT BRITAIN
in 11 on 13pt Old Style type
BY UNWIN BROTHERS LTD
LONDON AND WOKING

Contents

Introduction 9

Treatise entitled
'Complaint of a Stranger Exiled from Home' 21

1. Of Faith in God and His Attributes 83

2. Of Faith in Prophethood 87

3. Of Faith in the Next World 89

Appendix A 94

B 97

C 99

The superior numbers in the text refer to the notes at the end of each chapter.

All dates are given according to both the Moslem and Gregorian calendars; year 1 of the Moslem calendar is year 622 of the Gregorian.

Introduction

Sectarian hostility and doctrinal intolerance took a heavy toll of human lives, and created a crowded calendar of martyrs in mediaeval Islam no less than in Christianity. The most famous victim of outraged orthodoxy was al-Ḥallāj, 'martyr-mystic of Islam' as he was called by the late Louis Massignon, erudite and eloquent expositor of his tragedy, condemned by lawyers and theologians for alleged blasphemy, and executed with appalling cruelty in Baghdad on March 26, 922.[1] Next most celebrated mystic-martyr, undeservedly less well studied but coming increasingly into notice, was al-Suhrawardī al-Maqtūl, put to death by order of Saladin's son al-Malik al-Ẓāhir at Aleppo in 1191.[2]

In the following pages an account is given of the life, works and death of a third Sufi martyr, comparable in spiritual insight and tragic end with al-Ḥallāj and al-Suhrawardī, but overlooked largely by western scholarship, so much so that he has not been rated as qualifying for an entry in the voluminous *Encyclopaedia of Islam*, whether in its old or new edition; whilst Carl Brockelmann, the great bibliographer of Arabic literature, listed him not as a mystic but as a Shāfi'ī lawyer.[3] He has been rescued from total neglect first by the great Massignon,[4] then by his able pupil, the Moroccan Mohammed ben Abd el-Jalil;[5] next, bibliographically, by Fritz Meier;[6] and latterly, meritoriously, by the Persian editor Afif Osseiran.[7]

Abu 'l-Ma'ālī 'Abd Allāh ibn Abī Bakr Muḥammad ibn 'Alī ibn al-Ḥasan ibn 'Alī al-Miyānajī, known as 'Ain al-Quḍāt al-Hamadhānī, was born at Hamadhan in 492/1098.[8] He came of a learned stock, hailing originally from Miyana in Azerbaijan, a township midway between Maragha and Tabriz.[9] His grandfather was Qāḍī of Hamadhan, who there met a martyr's death; his father also came to a violent end.[10] Hamadhan was an ancient city, situated in central Persia in the shadow of Mt. Alwand, capital of the Medes and Achaemenids, long before the Arab conquest and the coming of Islam. By the second half of the fifth/eleventh century it had developed into a prosperous trading centre, part of the wide dominions of the Saljūqs. In 494/1100 it was sacked by the military,[11] for whatever reason, and perhaps it was under these circumstances that 'Ain al-Quḍāt, then a child of three years, lost his grandfather.

The meagre biographical notices which we possess say nothing of the childhood and education of 'Ain al-Quḍāt. That he was thoroughly schooled in the Arabic and Islamic sciences, and that he exhibited unusual precocity, may be reasonably deduced from his own writings, especially the work here translated, in which he speaks of his rare accomplishments with disarming naivety. ('It is no wonder that I am envied, seeing that I composed as a mere youth, sucking the udders of little more than twenty years, books which baffle men of fifty and sixty to understand, much less to compile and compose.')[12] Indeed, the fluency and elegance of his writings in Arabic attest his brilliance in classical studies; though to be sure, he was no more than following in this respect a tradition long established amongst Persian scholars. It can therefore be taken as certain that before his conversion to Sufism, 'Ain al-Quḍāt had completely mastered Arabic grammar, philology and literary history, Koranic exegesis, the sciences of Traditions of the Prophet, theology, jurisprudence (he favoured the Shāfi'ī school, and early qualified for appointment as Qāḍī[13]), as well as logic and philosophy—in short, all those branches of knowledge whose technical terms he rattles off with such effortless ease.[14] He began to compose original works seemingly from a very tender age; the treatise on which his accusers fastened when they came to charge him with heresy was apparently written in his fourteenth year.[15] This work has perished, along with his poetical compositions, and numerous other books on various subjects whose titles he gives us.[16]

'Ain al-Quḍāt states that he abandoned secular studies at the approach of puberty and manhood, when he 'went forth in quest of the religious sciences' and busied himself with 'treading the path of the Sufis'.[17] So he writes in the treatise here translated, his final work; ten years earlier he had recorded his conversion in more detail.[18] There he informs us that he was twenty-one when he compiled his monograph on the true nature of prophesy.[19] During the ensuing three years 'the Divine grace poured down upon me all manner of esoteric knowledge and precious revelations impossible to describe'.[20] He had been 'upon the very brink of hell-fire, had not God rescued me therefrom by His grace and favour'.[21] His study of the books of theology only increased his bewilderment and confusion. From this perilous state he was rescued, thanks to God's grace, by the perusal of the writings of the Proof of Islam, Abū Ḥāmid Muḥammad ibn Muḥammad al-Ghazālī, a study which occupied him nigh on four years, and delivered him out of error and blindness. When 'Ain al-Quḍāt wrote these words, so reminiscent of al-Ghazālī's own account of his conversion,[22] he was twenty-four, the year was 516/1122, and the great Abū Ḥāmid al-Ghazālī had been dead eleven years.

The writings of al-Ghazālī, and especially his masterwork the *Iḥyā' 'ulūm al-dīn*, exercised such a powerful influence on 'Ain al-Quḍāt that, as he states, 'the eye of spiritual vision began to open—and I do not mean intellectual vision'.[23] So he remained for nearly a year. Then it so happened that Abū Ḥāmid's brother, Abu 'l-Futūḥ Aḥmad al-Ghazālī, came to Hamadhan; and in less than twenty days' attendance on him his spiritual transformation was completed. Thereafter, until Aḥmad's death in 520/1126, the two continued in constant contact, always by correspondence, and from time to time by meeting. Aḥmad was a more rapt mystic than his brother, and his writings, above all the Persian *Sāwaniḥ* on spiritual love, affected Persian Sufism profoundly for centuries.[24] 'Ain al-Quḍāt informs us that his father was also present at Aḥmad's circle, and joined in the dancing which accompanied the meditation.[25]

We have the names of two other men who played a part in 'Ain al-Quḍāt's spiritual education. Jāmī informs us,[26] on the authority of one of 'Ain al-Quḍāt's letters, that one of his teachers was Abū 'Abd Allāh Muḥammad ibn Ḥamawaih al-Juwainī, learned in both the exoteric and the esoteric sciences, and author of a Sufi book entitled *Salwat al-ṭālibīn*. (Ibn Ḥamawaih died in 617/1220 according to the bibliographer Ḥajjī Khalīfa.[27] Al-Yāfi'ī gives the same date[28] for Abu 'l-Ḥasan Muḥammad ibn 'Umar ibn 'Alī al-Juwainī. This, however, seems to be a different man.) The other teacher, named by 'Ain al-Quḍāt himself[29] and from him quoted by Jāmī,[30] was a certain Baraka—we have no information as to his other names. He appears to have belonged to the familiar type of little-educated Sufi; he was certainly alive in 520/1126, but no further information regarding him is forthcoming.[31]

Much of 'Ain al-Quḍāt's energies were devoted to writing; and it will be convenient to list here his books, whether lost or extant.

(1) *Risāla*, composed apparently in his fourteenth year.[32] Lost.
(2) *Qirā 'l-'āshī ilā ma'rifat al-'ūrān wa'l-a'āshī*, subject unknown. Lost.
(3) *al-Risālat al-'Alā'īya*, a brief tract. Lost.
(4) *al-Muftaladh min al-taṣrīf*, a brief tract on syntax. Lost.
(5) *Amālī 'l-ishtiyāq fī layālī 'l-firāq*. Lost.
(6) *Munyat al-ḥaisūb*, on arithmetic. Lost.

(7) *Ghāyat al-baḥth 'an ma'nā 'l-ba'th*, on the true nature of prophesy, composed at the age of twenty-one.[33] Lost.

(8) *Ṣaulat al-bāzil al-amūn 'alā 'bn al-labūn*. Lost.

(9) *Nuzhat al-'ushshāq wa-nuhzat al-mushtāq*, 1000 erotic verses. Lost.

(10) *al-Madkhal ilā 'l-'arabīya wa-riyāḍat 'ulūmihā 'l-adabīya*, on belles-lettres, incomplete. Lost.

(11) *Tafsīr ḥaqā'iq al-Qur'ān*, esoteric commentary on the Koran, incomplete. Lost.

(12) *Risāla-yi Jamālī*, a brief tract on prophesy. Extant.[34]

(13) *Zubdat al-ḥaqā'iq*, on philosophy and theology, composed at the age of twenty-four. Extant and published.[35]

(14) *Tamhīdāt*, on mysticism, composed in 521/1127.[36] Extant and published.[37]

(15) *Maktūbāt*, letters. Extant.[38]

(16) *Shakwā 'l-gharīb*, apologia, composed in 525/1131. Extant, published and translated.[39]

The following works have also been ascribed to 'Ain al-Quḍāt.

(17) *Sharḥ Kalimāt qiṣār Bābā Ṭāhir*, a glossary of Ṣūfī terms. Extant.[40]

(18) *Risāla-yi Yazdān-shinākht*, on the knowledge of God. Extant.[41]

(19) *Risāla-yi Lawā'iḥ*, on mystical love. Extant and published.[42]

The reputation of 'Ain al-Quḍāt as a man of God soon attracted to him a large following; and his few remaining years were divided between oral teaching and instruction by correspondence. 'Every day', he writes, 'I hold forth to the people in seven or eight sessions on various learned topics, in each of which I speak not less than a thousand words.'[43]

At the same time he sometimes passed two or three months in exhausted recuperation. He married, and had at least one son.[44] His fame as a saint grew all the greater as miracles began to be attributed to him, including the raising of the dead.[45]

All this could not fail to provoke the orthodox theologians to envy and hostility. The war between the ulema and the Sufis had been raging for some three centuries; and despite the irenic efforts of a succession of mystical writers culminating in the gigantic work of Abū Ḥāmid al-Ghazālī, the battle raged on for long years thereafter and claimed its toll of martyrs. The nature of the charges brought against 'Ain al-Quḍāt will be discussed presently. For the moment it suffices to sketch, in the few details available, the last months of his life.

The ulema laid a formal complaint against 'Ain al-Quḍāt before the Saljūqid vizier of Iraq, named Abu 'l-Qāsim Qiwām al-Dīn Nāṣir ibn 'Alī al-Dargazīnī, a man of evil reputation as a bloodthirsty tyrant.[46] He threw the mystic into prison in Baghdad; there 'Ain al-Quḍāt composed the apologia here translated. After some months' detention in Baghdad he was sent back to his native Hamadham. There, on the night of the arrival of the Saljūq Sulṭān Maḥmūd (reigned 511–25/1118–31),[47] he was put to death in barbarous circumstances.[48] So ended, on 6–7 Jumādā II 525/6–7 May 1131, at the age of 33, this man of rare genius: intellectual, mystic, saint and martyr.

The charges of heresy brought by his accusers are listed in some detail by 'Ain al-Quḍāt in his apologia. The first offence was his attitude to the nature of prophecy, 'the appearance of which depended upon the manifestation of a stage beyond the stage of reason'.[49] He goes on, 'Philosophers deny such states because they are imprisoned in the narrow defile of reason. The term "prophet" for them means a man who has attained the farthest degree of reason.[50] That, however, has nothing in common with faith in prophethood. . . . Contemporary theologians have disapproved of me on this account amongst others, thinking that to claim there is a stage beyond the stage of reason is to bar the way to the common people to faith in prophecy. . . . Now I do not claim that faith in prophecy is dependent upon the appearance of a stage beyond the stage of reason. What I claim is rather that the inner nature of prophecy indicates a stage beyond the stage of sainthood, and that sainthood indicates a stage beyond the stage of reason.'[51]

All this is perfectly in accord with what 'Ain al-Quḍāt set out in his *Zubdat al-ḥaqā'iq*.[52] His further claim, that the views he expressed are no different from those expounded by Abū Ḥāmid al-Ghazālī, also approximates to the truth, allowing for the well-known difficulty of determining al-Ghazālī's final position.[53] In the *Tamhīdāt*, however, 'Ain al-Quḍāt advances notions regarding the prophetic teaching on the life after death which are completely at variance with orthodoxy, and with his credal position as put forth in the concluding section of the apologia. 'Seek the tomb within yourself . . . The human nature of a man is all the tomb . . . The interrogation of Munkar and Nakīr are likewise within the self . . . Ibn Sīnā, God have mercy upon him, expounded this idea in the words, "Munkar is the evil action and Nakīr is the good action . . .". The Pathway (over which all men must pass at the Last Judgement) must also be sought within the self . . . The Balance is the reason . . . Paradise and Hell are likewise with you, and must be sought within one's inner self . . .'[54] These heterodox notions indeed accord with the notorious teachings of Ibn Sīnā [Avicenna].[55] As for al-Ghazālī, he counted as heresy to be punished by execution the denial of the resurrection of the body. The assertion that a physical Hell, Paradise and the houris are 'mere parables coined for the common people . . . is contrary to the belief of all Moslems'.[56]

'Ain al-Quḍāt's second grave offence was his speaking of 'the need of the neophyte for a spiritual instructor to conduct him to the path of truth'. His accusers interpreted him as 'being in line with the doctrine of the Ismailis, understanding me to subscribe to the belief in the infallible Imam'.[57] This misconstruction of his teachings is particularly obtuse, having regard to what 'Ain al-Quḍāt wrote on the subject in the *Zubdat al-ḥaqā'iq*[58] and the *Tamhīdāt*;[59] there he departed in no way from the tenets of many Sufis before him.[60] In his (as yet unpublished) *Letters* he goes much farther in demanding total obedience of the disciple; though even then he is not without precedents.[61]

The third grave accusation brought against 'Ain al-Quḍāt was tantamount to a charge of pantheism. This attack fastened on his 'statement regarding the Maker of the world, that He is "the source and origin of being", that He is "the All", that He is "the Real Being", and that all other than He is, as regards its essence, vain, perishing, passing away, non-existent, and having being only in so far as the Eternal Omnipotence sustains its existence'.[62] (A side issue was the charge that these phrases implied that the world existed from eternity, a damnable heresy disproved at length by 'Ain al-Quḍāt elsewhere.[63] A further alleged offence was 'an allusion to the doctrine that God has no knowledge of details'.[64] The accusers thus completed the tally of three heresies specified by al-Ghazālī as qualifying for instant execution.[65]) 'Ain al-Quḍāt defends himself against the charge of pantheism by invoking the famous Sufi doctrine of *fanā'*, the passing away of contingent being into the Being of God.[66] This doctrine had indeed by his time become so central and integral a part of Sufi teaching, that it is a little surprising that 'Ain al-Quḍāt should have been specifically taken to task on account of it. Yet it must be remembered that strict orthodoxy never became reconciled to a theory which, in its extreme form, appeared little different from the heinous heresy of incarnationism (*ḥulūl*), of God indwelling in man.[67]

The translation of 'Ain al-Quḍāt's apologia here offered has been based upon the two editions so far published. The *editio princeps*, printed in the *Journal Asiatique* (Paris, January–March 1930, pages 1–76, and April–June 1930, pages 193–297), was the work of the Moroccan scholar Mohammed ben Abd al-Jalil, and was accompanied by a valuably annotated translation. The second edition, prepared by the Persian scholar Afif Osseiran together with the *Zubdat al-ḥaqā'iq* and the *Tamhīdāt*, along with most excellent prefaces and indexes, came out at Teheran in 1962. The present writer's debt to both these pioneers is both obvious and great.

Notes

1. For bibliography, see now *E.I.*² III 99–104.
2. For a recent annotated account, see Seyyed Hossein Nasr, *Three Muslim Sages* (Harvard University Press, 1964), 52–82, 147–56.
3. See *G.A.L.* I 391, Suppl. I 674–75.
4. See references in *Textes inédits* (Paris, 1929).
5. See below.
6. See 'Stambuler Handschriften dreier persischer Mystiker' in *Der Islam* (1937), 1–42.
7. See below.
8. Osseiran, preface to *Tamhīdāt*, 45–6, with references.
9. Yāqūt, *Mu'jam al-buldān* (Cairo, 1323/1906), VIII 220.
10. Abd el-Jalil, 6, with fn. 7.
11. See *E.I.*² III 105.
12. See translation below.
13. Abd el-Jalil, 8.
14. See below.

15. But Abd el-Jalil, 7, fn. 2, challenges the validity of the text on this point (see below, 30) proposing to emend 'twenty' to 'ten' and tentatively (but see 16, fn. 1) identifying the offending *Risāla* with the *Zubdat al-ḥaqa'iq*. Publication of the latter text has now strengthened this hypothesis; see Osseiran, preface to *Shakwā 'l-gharīb*.
16. See below.
17. See below.
18. *Zubdat al-ḥaqā'iq*, 4–7.
19. *Ibid.*, 4, referring to the *Ghāyat al-baḥth 'an ma'nā 'l-ba'th*. Abd el-Jalil, 261, wrongly translates *ba'th* as 'résurrection'.
20. *Zubda*, 4.
21. *Ibid.*, 6.
22. *Al-Munqidh min al-ḍalāl*; see W. M. Watt, *The Faith and Practice of al-Ghazālī* (London, 1953).
23. *Zubda*, 7.
24. See *E.I.*[2] II 1041–42, with bibliography.
25. See *Tamhīdāt*, 250–51.
26. *Nafaḥāt al-uns* (Teheran, 1337 AHS/1949), 414.
27. *Kashf al-ẓunūn* (Istanbul, 1943), col. 999.
28. *Mir'āt al-janān*, IV 39.
29. See Osseiran, preface to *Tamhīdāt*, 61.
30. *Nafaḥāt*, 416.
31. Osseiran, 62.
32. But see note 15 above.
33. See note 19.
34. See Osseiran, 2, with fn. 3.
35. Teheran, 1962 (Publications de l'Université de Téhéran, No. 695).
36. See Osseiran, 17.
27. See note 35.
38. *G.A.L.* Suppl. I 675; Osseiran, 9–12.
39. See below.
40. *G.A.L.* Suppl. I 770; Osseiran, 35.
41. Osseiran, 36–9.
42. Osseiran, 39–44. Teheran (ed. R. Farmanesh), 1958.
43. Osseiran, 77.
44. *Ibid.*, 78.

45. Abd el-Jalil, 9.
46. Abd el-Jalil spells Darguzīnī, but see Yāqūt IV 54.
47. *E.I.*[1] III 132–33.
48. Crucified or burnt alive; see biographical sources (Abd el-Jalil, 18; Osseiran, preface to *Shakwā*, 1–5).
49. See translation below.
50. For the various theories of prophecy, see F. Rahman, *Prophecy in Islam* (London, 1958).
51. See below.
52. *Zubda*, 3–4, 31.
53. See F. Rahman, *op. cit.*, 94–9.
54. *Tamhīdāt*, 288–90.
55. See my *Revelation and Reason in Islam* (London, 1957). 50–2.
56. *Ibid.*, 62.
57. See below, 34. For the Ismaili position, see my *Revelation*, 70–1, with references.
58. See 72–4.
59. See 10.
60. See R. A. Nicholson, *The Mystics of Islam* (London, 1914), 32–5.
61. Extracts in Osseiran, preface to *Shakwā*, 12–16.
62. See below.
63. See *Zubda*, 42–64.
64. See below.
65. See my *Revelation*, 62.
66. For this doctrine, see e.g. Hujwīrī, *Kashf al-maḥjūb* (tr. Nicholson), 241–6; A. H. Abdel-Kader, *The Life, Personality and Writings of al-Junayd* (London, 1962), 152–9.
67. See *E.I.*[2] III 570–1.

TREATISE ENTITLED

'Complaint of a Stranger Exiled from Home'

Servants of God, is it not true,
Where'er I go, whate'er I do,
I cannot aught, except there be
A Watcher watching over me?

This is a flash issued to the outstanding scholars and renowned servants—may God perpetuate their shadows outstretched over the dwellers in the farthest horizons, and may all the regions of the earth never cease to be most brilliantly illumined by their lights—by one in exile from his motherland, and afflicted by the trials and tribulations of time. His eyelids are ever beset by sleeplessness, and trepidation is the constant companion of his pillow, with prolonged weeping, and sighs and lamentations; anxiety grips the whole of his heart; his soul entire is inflamed with grief, whose repeated onsets his heart's core can no longer endure. His heart, consumed by the fire of separation, burns with yearning for his friends and brothers; the burning pangs of love ever blaze in his bowels, and the marks thereof appear ever more clearly with the passing days. His only companions are the stars, to which he whispers with flooding tears:

What, prison bars and iron chains,
And yearning's flames, and exile pains,
And sundering far from those I love?
What mighty anguish these must prove![1]

Moreover, not a friend is there to whom he may disclose

some part at least of his sorrows, and with whom he may find relief from what he is suffering at the hand of his brothers; no brother to whom he may complain of the vicissitudes of fortune, and in whom he may look for succour against the hardships he is enduring. So he is wakeful through the long night, and passes his day as the poet describes:

This way I look and that, yet see
No person truly loving me,
Whilst in the house how many throng
Who only seek to do me wrong.

And when the tightening of his breast becomes too severe, he assuages his sorrow by reciting these verses:

Long separation leads at last
My footsteps to a dwelling fast
Of exile where, if so I will,
I meet a man who meets me ill.

With him in folly I compete
Till I am hailed 'the fool complete';
Had he possessed of sense a glim,
I would have sought to outreason him.[2]

Likewise, when he recalls the ox-eyes and nenuphars of Arwand,[3] and Hamadhan where the ladies of the curtained canopies[4] suckled him, his tears run down his cheeks, his breast is rent and his heart is broken; he writhes in the agony of his grief, whilst yearningly he recites:

Ah, would I knew if ever more
My eyes shall light upon where soar
The summits of the massifs twain
Of Arwand, hard by Hamadhan!

'Complaint of a Stranger Exiled from Home'

That land where amulets were hung
About my neck, when I was young,
And I was suckled at the breast
With milk abundantly expressed.[5]

When he remembers his brothers, the words of Ibn al-Ṭathrīya[6] are constantly upon his tongue:

Would that the breezes might convey
To us the words that they would say,
And speed thereafter, by and by,
From us to them with our reply—

Missives that find us ailing sore,
And have the power to restore
Our flagging spirits, now accursed
By love's intolerable thirst.

Then he chants these lines of Ḥabīb,[7] the plaintive sigh of a lover passionate and forlorn:

Delight no more to us displays
The beauty of her unveiled face,
Not since amid the twisted sands
Love's youthful joy slipped from our hands.[8]

No wonder is it that fortitude should be defeated, and that the breast should be too constricted to conceal its secret. For the man afflicted, when his sighs mount up, his tears betray all his secrets. A man has no power against what surpasses his strength to endure. How justly the poet described this situation:

I hid my passion, that black day
We parted, and went each his way,

And yet my sighs spread far and wide
The secret that they could not hide.

My breast was well nigh rent in twain
By that explosion of my pain,
As ever sigh on deep-drawn sigh
Betrayed what I was riven by.

Pitiable indeed is the man who is beset by crowding cares, and cannot find any to console him; it was to such a plight that Bashshār[9] referred:

So I divulged to 'Amr a part
Of what was seething in my heart,
Pouring into his cup to drain
A sample of my bitter pain.

For one must needs complain at last
To one whose faith is true and fast,
When the pent secrets of the soul
Burst suddenly uncontrollable.

Shall he who has found a companion deem the way ahead rugged? Shall he who has chanced upon a congenial neighbour regret the remoteness of his abode? Consider the lines of Dhu 'l-Qurūḥ[10] composed in the agony of his soul:

Dear neighbour of mine, we dwell
House close to house, truth to tell,
And I shall abide secure
As long as 'Asīb, be sure.

Dear neighbour of mine, we twain
As exiles must here remain,
And the exile (is it not true?)
To the exile is kinsman, too.

'Complaint of a Stranger Exiled from Home'

So, if you accept my love,
Our affection shall constant prove;
But if you reject me, then
The exile is exile again.

The verses of Ibn Ḥujr[11] recall to my mind the words of Ṭahmān b. 'Amr:[12]

How well-beloved are you,
By God, if you but knew,
How dear, you mountains twain,
With your cool, shadowy train!

Your water too, so sweet
That if I drank of it
When fever wracked my frame,
It would assuage its flame.

The man of 'Abs and I
We both in Madhhij lie,
Two exiles riven far
From home, yet comrades are.

Hard-done-by exiles we,
Our chief anxiety
Is to urge on apace
Our mounts from place to place.

Who sees our night's abode
Where we cast down our load,
That man must know, mark you,
That we are lions true.

The shy, averted glance
Was ne'er our natural stance,
But here in Madhhij we
Can naught but exiles be.

Methinks I see the Iraqi caravan arriving at Hamadhan, and setting down their loads on the slopes of Māwashān.[13] The heights and valleys there are verdant green, bedecked by spring in raiment which all other lands would envy. Her flowers waft abroad as it were the scent of musk, her rivers flow with crystal-limpid water. The travellers alight amid elegant gardens, and betake themselves to the shade of leafy trees. They begin to chant over and over again this verse, and they cooing like doves and warbling like nightingales:

O Hamadhan, may copious rain
Water abundantly thy plain,
Nor may fresh showers ever fail,
O Māwashān, thy fertile vale.[14]

Then their brothers go out to meet them, and question them, old and young alike, concerning our state of affairs. The hearts reach the throats,[15] and their tears invade their eyes, and they cry:

'Where is our sister's son?' demand
The women of our quarter, and,
'Give us some tidings of the man,
God greet and guard your caravan!

'In Allah's keeping may it dwell!
Have you within your land to tell
Of one right noble, keeping faith
With noble comrades to the death?

'For he whom you have left behind
In your ancestral land confined—
He is a youth whose absence long
Has filled our hearts with passion strong.

'Complaint of a Stranger Exiled from Home'

'Does your Baghdad make him forget
Arwand, his spring encampment, yet?
A sorry bargain he has had
Who barters Arwand for Baghdad!'

O may my soul their ransom be!
If they but heard what now I see,
Each heaving throat would fling aside
The string of pearls about it tied.[16]

How indeed should I forget my brothers, how should I not yearn for my homeland? For the Messenger of God, God bless him and grant him peace, declared, 'Love for one's homeland is a part of faith'. It is no secret that love of one's homeland is compounded into the very nature of man:

Of all God's creatures, those I love
The dearest betwixt Man'aj rove
And Lailā's hot and stormy plain—
May the clouds deluge it with rain!

'Twas in those lands of mother earth
My midwives took me at my birth,
There first, in all the world's wide rims,
The soft dust touched my tender limbs.[17]

When Uṣail al-Khuzā'ī came from Mecca into the presence of God's Messenger (God bless him and grant him peace), the latter said to him, 'Describe Mecca to us'. So Uṣail proceeded to describe the city. When he pronounced the words, 'Its mimosas are thickly intertwined, and its schoenantha are freshly sprouting', the Prophet said, 'O Uṣail, suffer the heart to regain its tranquillity'.

The Prophet (God bless him) heard Bilāl[18] reciting:

Ah, would I knew if ever I
One night shall in a valley lie
Surrounded by the sweet perfume
Of panic grass and juncus bloom!

Shall I one day come down to taste
Mijanna's waters in the waste,
Or shall Mount Shāma yet reveal
Itself to me, or Mount Ṭafīl?

The Prophet said, 'Do you then yearn so, son of a negress?'

If therefore such men as these yearned for their homelands, and gave expression on their tongues to the feelings concealed within their hearts and their deepest love, how then should it be with me, feeble as I am, in that I am sorely tried by exile, and most severe distress, the affliction of imprisonment, and perpetual grief:

What though the heart in me
Of steel should fashioned be,
For all its toughness fast
That steel would melt at last.

And if the sable crow
Endured my grief and woe,
And shared my worries, lo!
'Twould turn as white as snow.

For cares have crowded in upon me, and have bent their necks towards me; my bowels have become a dwelling-place for them, so that consolation cannot find a way unto them. I have come to regard my enemy as if I were his friend; for the misfortunes of destiny have loaded me with a burden I cannot endure. If such a load were laid upon the mountains, they would be split asunder; if upon hard and solid rocks, they would be broken to pieces:

'Complaint of a Stranger Exiled from Home'

If this that weighs upon my bones
Assailed the rocks, 'twould split those stones!
Or did it smite the winds that roar,
Their whistle would be heard no more.

Yes indeed; but this branch of learning,[19] though it is more appealing to human nature and is lighter on the ears, yet I have bidden it farewell and departed from it ever since I approached puberty and manhood. I have gone forth in quest of the religious sciences, and have busied myself with treading the path of the Sufis; and how foul it is for a Sufi to turn away from a thing and then to return to it, and apply himself to it with all his heart. It is no secret that a man who has plunged deeply into the sciences, and has become apprised of their hidden mysteries, does not revert to the ABC in order to succour idiots. The intelligent man knows well that nature rebels against change, and that he who challenges nature is vanquished thereby. When, then, shall the object of disdain ever become the object of desire?

A Bedouin gave admirable expression to his situation in the verses which follow. His heart had turned again passionately to the desert life. The settled folk and the dwellers in mud huts advised him to learn writing, whilst he yearned longingly for the Bedouin ways; till finally he resumed his accustomed vagrancy. He spoke thus regarding the 'ignorance' which had overcome him:

I met some Refugees, who instructed me
To read three lines inscribed successively,
The Book of God upon pure parchment penned
And verses which distinctly did descend.

Then they traced out the alphabet, and said,
'Now learn your ABC and XYZ'.
But what have I to do with scripts and spelling,
The inheritance of sons from daughters telling?

But now I will return to my purposed object, to acquaint the men of learning—may their sweet fountains ever be accessible to those who would drink of them, and their broad meadows remain the grazing-grounds of those that seek for fodder—of the exact truth of my case and the reality of my situation, of the sufferings brought on me by destiny such as I had never imagined in my wildest dreams. I beg them only to lend me their ears, that I may assail them with the lamentations of a bleeding heart, quoting to them the lines of Abū Tammām al-Ṭā'ī:

You mighty men who hear my ditty,
Incline towards me in your pity;
A mighty thirst burns me complete,
And you are fountains pure and sweet.[20]

May God guard him who turns his ear to me, that I may disclose to him some part of the crimes committed against me by the hands of fate.

For a group of contemporary theologians—may God succour them perfectly and ease their way to the best of both worlds; may He remove all rancour from their breasts, and furnish them with rectitude in all their affairs—have disapproved of me on account of certain phrases published in a treatise which I composed twenty years ago. My purpose in inditing it was to explain certain states claimed by the Sufis, the appearance of which depended upon the manifestation of a stage beyond the stage of reason. Philosophers deny such states because they are imprisoned in the narrow defile of reason. The term 'prophet' for them means a man who has attained the furthest degree of reason. That, however, has nothing in common with faith in prophethood. Prophethood in fact consists in a variety of perfections which supervene in a stage beyond the stage of sainthood. The stage of sainthood itself transcends the stage of reason.[21]

By the stage of sainthood we mean that it is possible for a saint to have revealed to him truths which the man of reason cannot be conceived of as attaining or stumbling upon by means of his natural equipment. Thus, it was revealed to Abū Bakr al-Ṣiddīq (God be well pleased with him) in his last illness that his wife would give birth to a daughter, so that he said to 'Ā'isha, 'They are your two sisters'; whereas at that time 'Ā'isha had only one sister, Asmā'.[22] It was thus realized that this had been revealed to him. Similarly, in the same illness someone said to him, 'Shall we call a doctor for you?'[23] He replied, 'I have with me the Doctor of all doctors, Who has said, "I perform whatsoever I desire"'.[24] So again it was realised that his death had been revealed to him.

So too 'Umar (God be well pleased with him) cried out, whilst that day preaching in the pulpit, 'O Sāriya, the mountain!', Sāriya being in command of his army at Nihāwand.[25] The fact that he was fully aware of the situation of Sāriya and his men, though he was in Medina and they at Nihāwand, and that his voice reached Sāriya, as also that Abū Bakr knew that his wife would give birth to a daughter, and that he would die of his present illness—these are noble truths and sublime affairs the likes of which could not conceivably be attained by the equipment of mere reason, but rather by a divine light transcending reason.

Similarly it is related that a certain Companion[26] entered the presence of 'Uthmān, having on the way looked at a woman. 'Uthmān said to him, 'What ails one of you, that he enters my presence having in his eyes the mark of adultery?' The man said to him, 'What, is there revelation then, after the death of God's Messenger?' 'No,' replied 'Uthmān, 'but intuition, demonstration, a true clairvoyance. Have you not heard that God's Messenger (God bless him and his family) said, "Fear the clairvoyance of the believer, for he sees by the light of God".'[27]

'Alī (peace be upon him) came out of his house, on the day on which he was killed,[28] and proceeded to recite over and over again:

> *Gird well your breast for death today,*
> *For death lurks surely on your way,*
> *And do not fret that you must die*
> *Since death doth in your valley lie.*

When Harim b. Ḥaiyān came to Kufa to visit Uwais al-Qaranī, having set out from Mecca with this sole purpose, he went on enquiring for him until at last he encountered him. After Harim had greeted him Uwais replied, 'And on you be peace, Harim b. Ḥaiyān'. Harim cried out, 'How did you know my name and the name of my father, seeing that I never saw you before today, nor you me?' Uwais answered, 'I was informed by the All-knowing, the All-aware. My spirit recognized your spirit the moment my soul spoke to your soul. Spirits have souls as bodies do. Believers surely recognize one another.'[29]

My purpose in citing these examples is to show that such things cannot be attained by the equipment of mere reason. Contemporary theologians have disapproved of me on this account amongst others, thinking that to claim there is a stage beyond the stage of reason is to bar the way to the common people to faith in prophecy, inasmuch as it is reason that proves the veracity of the Prophets.

Now I do not claim that faith in prophecy is dependent upon the appearance of a stage beyond the stage of reason. What I claim is rather that the inner nature of prophecy indicates a stage beyond the stage of sainthood, and that sainthood indicates a stage beyond the stage of reason, as I have pointed out above. The nature of a thing is one thing, and the means of realizing it is another: it is possible for a man possessed of reason to reach by way of reason belief in the existence of a stage which he has not yet attained personally. Thus, a man may be deprived of the taste for poetry, and yet he may come to recognize the existence of something in the man possessing such taste, whilst at the same time he must confess total ignorance of the nature of that thing.

Yet the pronouncements[30] of which they have disapproved in me are all to be found, in word and meaning, in the books of the Imam, the Proof of Islam, Abū Ḥāmid al-Ghazālī.[31] Such is the case with our statement regarding the Maker of the world, that He is 'the source and origin of being', that He is 'the All', that He is 'the Real Being', and that all other than He is, as regards its essence, vain, perishing, passing away, non-existent, and having being only in so far as the Eternal Omnipotence sustains its existence. All these expressions occur in many places in the *Iḥyā' 'ulūm al-dīn*, the *Mishkāt al-anwār wa-miṣfāt al-asrār*, and the *al-Munqidh min al-ḍalāl wa'l-mufṣiḥ 'an al-aḥwāl*, all of which are works of al-Ghazālī,[32] God have mercy upon him.

Our statement that God is 'the origin and source of being' is equivalent to our saying that He is the creator of all things. Whoever interprets it otherwise is in error, and not the maker of the statement. In the case of summary expressions, for their explanation recourse is to be had to the one issuing these, not to his vexatious adversary. A man lies hidden under his own tongue, and not under the tongues of his enemies. I do not deny that our expressions 'the origin of being' and 'the source of being' are summary terms capable of various interpretations, some false and some true. What is certain is that al-Ghazālī intended only that:

Came the alarmists with supplies
Of wild conjectures and plain lies,
To catch you unawares; from me
You get true news and certainty.[33]

How can such allegations stick? The impartial observer will discover in my treatise such things as would cause him to realize that my adversary is indeed vexatious. For if my enemy chooses to understand from my expressions 'origin of being' and 'source of being' an implication that the world is eternal, it is a fact that in that treatise I have devoted nearly ten leaves to assert that the world was created in time, a view which I have supported with conclusive proofs.[34] If my enemy, moreover, understands from what I have written an allusion to the doctrine that God has no knowledge of details, I have demonstrated that God does indeed have such knowledge in a manner leaving the intelligent man no room for doubt.

Another matter over which they have criticized me concerns certain chapters wherein I have spoken of the need of the neophyte for a spiritual instructor to conduct him to the path of truth and to guide him on the straight road, so that he may not stray from the right way.[35] A sound Tradition informs us that God's Messenger (God bless him) said, 'Whoever dies without an imam, dies the death of a pagan'. Abū Yazīd al-Bisṭāmī[36] said, 'If a man has no master, his imam is Satan.' 'Amr b. Sinān al-Manbijī,[37] one of the great Sufi shaikhs, said, 'A man who has not been to school with a master, such a man is an imposter'. The Sufi expositors of the true reality are unanimous in declaring that he who has no shaikh is without religion.

This was what I meant to say in the chapters in question. My adversary, however, had chosen to interpret my words as being in line with the doctrine of the Ismailis, understanding me to subscribe to the belief in the infallible Imam. Yet how could he arrive at such a vexatious misconstruction, seeing that the second chapter of my treatise is devoted to demonstrating the existence of Almighty God by way of rational speculation and incontrovertible proof? It is well known that the Ismailis reject rational speculation, asserting that the way to the knowledge of Almighty God is the Prophet, or the infallible Imam. Yet how can the adversary allow the like of such procedures, seeing that God's Messenger (God bless him and grant him peace) said, 'You people who believe with their tongues, and whose hearts faith has not yet entered, do not backbite the Muslims, and do not ferret out their secrets. Whose ferrets out his brother's secret, God will ferret out his; and whosoever's secret God ferrets out, He will put him to shame, even in the depths of his house.' Moreover, how can it be permissible for scholars to say such things, and to follow these paths in dealing with a fellow-Muslim, much less a scholar like themselves, seeing that the Lord of the Prophets Muḥammad (God bless him and grant him peace) said, 'Who reports what his eyes have seen and his ears have heard, God will inscribe him amongst those who desire that turpitude should spread abroad amongst the believers. There awaits them a painful punishment.'[38]

Yet they have not confined themselves to mere disapproval of my writings; they have further attributed to me on this account every foul vice, and have prevailed upon the authorities to put me to the most utter shame.

They've whispered tales most heinous
Amongst the tribe regarding us;
They who kept peace with us, now those
Declare themselves our open foes.

Such is Almighty God's way of old with His servants; the superior man is always envied, and becomes the target for all manner of injuries inflicted by the common people and the theologians.

'God has a son'—so it is trumpeted;
'The Prophet is a soothsayer', it's said.
Since God has not escaped the stubborn lie
Of men, neither His Prophet, how should I?

Let it be granted that those with ulterior aims have in fact found in the concise expressions of my treatise scope for objection, yet what have they to say regarding the clear terms it contains which are not open to interpretation? I am reminded here of the verses:

Can you with outstretched hands efface
The stars from heaven's unmeasured space,
Or can your fingers veil so soon
The radiance of the crescent moon?

Then leave the lions to their sleep
And quiet in their coverts deep,
Nor hazard heedlessly your blood
To satiate their thirsty brood.

Why should I deem that so remote, when the Koran that speaks the truth declares:

In Joseph and his brethren were signs for those who ask questions.[39]

It is no secret that it was envy that incited Joseph's brethren to slay him, when they saw that he was dearer to their father than they. Withal, they declared that their father Jacob (upon whom be peace) was in error, as is related of them in the Koran:

Surely our father is
in manifest error.[40]

If the sons of prophets dared to act thus towards their brother and their father on account of envy, it is not surprising if men like ourselves should commit wrongs many times as great against total strangers. Abū Ṭālib al-Makkī[41] stated, God have mercy upon him, 'I have counted, against

Joseph's brothers, from their saying "Surely Joseph and his brother are dearer to their father than we" to God's saying "for they set small store by him",[42] more than forty sins, some small and some great. In a single word two, or three, or four sins may be combined; these I have deduced by a minute examination of the secrets of sins.'

Envy is one of the great and deadly sins; from it no man can escape, according to the dictum of God's Messenger (God bless him), 'There are three things from which no man can escape: suspicion, augury and envy'. In another version of this saying there exists the possibility of escape: 'There are three things from which few men escape.' The Prophet (peace be upon him) also said, 'Envy devours good deeds as fire devours brushwood'; 'Men shall enter hell-fire before the Judgement on account of six things—rulers through injustice, Arabs through chauvinism, landowners through pride, peasants through ignorance, merchants through fraud, and scholars through envy'; and, 'Envy wellnigh vanquishes destiny'. It was for this reason that Almighty God ordered Muḥammad to take refuge from it, saying, 'Say: I take refuge with the Lord of the Daybreak' down to 'and from the evil of an envier when he envies'.[43]

Why should I be concerned with the envious man and his malicious design? Is he not sufficiently punished by the suffering brought on him by this ignoble vice, and his enmity against the virtuous? It was on account of the baseness of this characteristic, and the hopeless error of the one corrupted by it, that the poet said:

Say unto him who envious is of me,
'Know you against whom you act unmannerly?
God and His works you impugn, being malcontent
With what God has for my small portion sent.
God has requited you by giving more
To me, and shutting in your face His door.'

It is no wonder that they envy me, in view of the poet's saying:

For chiefs to have a blackened name,
And to be envied, is no shame;
The butt of envious intent
Is like the pole that props the tent.

No sin lies against the man who is envied, for God Himself favoured him with His special grace, but for which the envier would not have longed to be like him. It is also no reproach to him who envies one outstanding, who leaves his competitors in the field of learning far behind him, and who treads underfoot the summits of the stars, so that he has become an object of pride to strangers and kinsmen alike. How far from perfection is he who treats the envious as his foes! The composer of these lines put the matter excellently:

Excuse the man who envies you
For being of the favoured few;
In cases of sublimity
The finest thing is jealously.

Moreover, my adversaries have attributed to me a pretence to prophethood, on account of my using certain technical terms of the Sufis such as 'annihilation'[44] and 'passing away':[45]

Because Umm Ja'far I adore
They beat me, and they beat me sore
With every stick that comes to view—
Even the kitchen ladle, too!

How icy bigotry can be, when it reaches such limits! How foul is envy, especially in a scholar, when it pushes him to such extremes! He will then not be ashamed to attribute to a fellow-Muslim—not to say a fellow-scholar—monstrous beliefs which would be scorned by not only Magians and Christians, who deny the mission of the Lord of the Prophets, but also Brahmins who deny the very principle of prophecy, and atheists who reject the Sender along with the Messengers.

They charge both me, and her as well,
With an abomination fell
Themselves are likelier to commit—
God grant them swift defeat in it!—

A thing which, by Muhammad's Lord
I swear, we have long since abhorred;
Then let them show some decency
Or, at the least, plain courtesy.[46]

Misrepresentations such as these are all too familiar to anyone who has consorted with theologians, and who has jostled scholars with his knees, so that he has come to distinguish between false and true. He has learned then to recognize invented doctrines and forged falsehoods, and has verified how the holy Fathers followed the straight path and kept to the true way. How apposite are the lines of al-Kūfī,[47] in which he demonstrated that the virtuous cannot be harmed by what envious ignoramuses may say:

And when you hear me held to blame
By one inferior in fame,
Take that true evidence to be
Of my superiority.

The poet seems to have been thinking of his predecessor and his outstandingly brilliant verses:

When God desires to publish wide
A virtue circumstances hide,
He grants to loose against it then
The biting tongues of envious men.[48]

Theologians are not ignorant of the fact that every department of learning has its own technical vocabulary agreed upon by those who specialize in it; the terms used in each department are only known to those who follow that path. Thus, it may well be that the grammarian does not know the technical terms of the genealogist, such as *people, tribe, sub-tribe, sub-sub-tribe, family, subdivision, appendage,* and *female heredity*. The genealogist similarly may not know the technical terms of the grammarian, such as *declinable, indeclinable, subject, predicate, clause compounded of verb and agent, determinate noun, indeterminate noun, intransitive, transitive, simple, compound, curtailed, direct object, associated accusative, inflected nouns,* and *uninflected nouns*. Likewise the morphologist may not know the terms of the scholastic theologian, such as *substance, accident, location, corpus, existence, motion, rest, combination, acquisition*. The scholastic theologian on his side may not know the terms of the morphologist, such as *triliteral, quadriliteral, hollow, defective, doubly weak, augmentation, permutation, contraction*—unless indeed he has studied both sciences together, and is familiar with both sets of terms. In the same way the lawyer may not know the terms of the traditionist, such as *weak, rejected, rare, well-attested, well-known*; whilst the traditionist may not know the lawyer's terms, *contract, right of pre-emption, laws of inheritance, dependence, oath of sexual abstention, divorce by estrangement, deed of manumission*. Mathematicians may not know the terms used by the specialists in first principles, such as *branch, root principle, cause, judgement, necessary, recommended, reprehended, forbidden, allowed, enlarged, narrowed, specified, optional, restricted, absolute, particular, general, abrogating, abrogated, conformity, independent judgement.* The specialist in first principles, too, may not know the mathematicians' terms, *multiplication, division, root, cube, incommensurable, commensurable, x, square, to the fourth power, to the sixth power.* The prosodist may not know what the logician means by *attribute, subject, negation, affirmation, categorical, conditional, confrontation, figure*; so, too, the logician may not know the prosodist's meaning when he speaks of *rope, peg, division, metre, last foot, long, protracted, simple, adjacent.*[49]

My object in expounding this principle has been to show that every science has men who devote themselves to it especially, and to whom it is necessary to have recourse if one wishes to ascertain the precise meaning of their technical terms. By the same means the Sufis also employ technical terms between themselves, the meanings of which are not known to others.

By *Sufis* I mean certain people who have turned with their inmost purpose to God, and have occupied themselves with following His path. The beginning of their way is struggle against the enemy, and remaining constant in the recollection of God. It is they who are promised right guidance on the road in the most mighty Book, as Almighty God says:

> *But those who struggle in Our cause, surely*
> *We shall guide them in Our ways.*[50]

So how can any man who has known nothing of 'struggle'[51] (which is the beginning of the Sufi way) except its name—how can he make free with their technical terms, the meanings of which only the adepts know? A man who knows nothing of jurisprudence but its name, how is it permissible for him to make free with expressions the meanings of which only the greatest lawyers know?

Those who followed the path of God in the former ages and first generations were not known by the name of Sufis. Sufi is an expression which came into fame during the third century. The first to be so named in Baghdad was 'Abdak al-Ṣūfī;[52] he was one of the greatest and most ancient shaikhs, and lived before Bishr b. al-Ḥārith al-Ḥāfī[53] and al-Sarī b. al-Mughallis al-Saqaṭī.[54]

Struggle is a simple noun, like *jurisprudence, medicine* and *grammar*. Just as the meanings of these words are known only to those who have studied these sciences to the point of comprehending alike their generalities and their details, so *struggle* is a science in its own right which is only known to those who have studied it thoroughly. It is this science which the *Iḥyā' 'ulūm al-dīn* enbraces from beginning to end. No work had been composed on this subject in the beginning of Islam, in my opinion, to rival the *Qūt al-qulūb* of Abū Ṭālib al-Makkī.

Then, when the student has mastered the science of *struggle*, that is of no avail to him without his actually *struggling* himself; just as it is not enough for the sick man to be ever so clever at medicine, without he swallows the loathsome-tasting remedy. Once the student has mastered the science of *struggle*, and has *struggled* in God's cause well and truly, then God will guide him on His road, and will teach him what he knew not, as the Almighty says:

> *If you fear God, He will assign*
> *you a salvation.*[55]

Ibn 'Abbās[56] interpreted, 'That is, a light whereby you may distinguish between truth and falsehood'. It is to this meaning that God refers elsewhere:

> *If you obey him, you will be guided.*[57]

'Complaint of a Stranger Exiled from Home'

And again:

> *Yet had the peoples of the cities believed and been godfearing, We would have opened upon them blessings from heaven.*[58]

This is the wisdom referred to in the words of Almighty God:

> *He gives the Wisdom to whomsoever He will, and whoso is given the Wisdom, has been given much good.*[59]

Wisdom is not the fruit of wordy discussion; on the contrary, it is the heritage of silence. So the Prophet (upon whom be peace) said, 'If you see a man silent, grave, then approach him, for he is being dictated (or, presented with) wisdom'—the two versions differ. 'The fear of the Lord is the beginning of wisdom', as the text of the Psalms testifies.[60]

No period in the history of Islam has been without a group who have discoursed on these sciences. Some have spoken on the science of the 'path', some on the science of 'attainment'. Some have addressed men in common, some have confined themselves to their companions in particular.

Al-Junaid[61] (God be well pleased with him) said, 'Our Master in the aforesaid affair, the one who referred to the contents of the heart, and pointed out the truths thereof, after our Prophet (God bless him and his family), is 'Alī b. Abī Ṭālib (upon whom be peace)'. Al-Junaid was questioned concerning 'Alī b. Abī Ṭālib (upon whom be peace) and his knowledge of the science of Sufism. He said, 'The Commander of the Faithful 'Alī b. Abī Ṭālib, had he been at leisure from the wars to attend to us, there would have been transmitted to us from him such secrets of this science as our hearts could not support. He was a man to whom had been given the science divine.'[62] Al-Junaid also said, 'Had I known that there was beneath the dome of heaven a science of Almighty

God more noble than this science on which we discourse with our companions and brothers, I would have applied myself to it most earnestly and sought it out'. Al-Junaid often recited:

The science of Sufism a science is
Such as no man can rightly claim it his
Except he be endowed with natural wit,
And have the gift of understanding it.

None can pretend its intimate to be
Save he has seen its inmost mystery;
And how can he who is deprived of sight
Aspire to contemplate the sun's great light?[63]

Al-Junaid and Aḥmad b. Wahb al-Zaiyāt[64] used to discourse together on the science of Sufism. Al-Junaid would derive profit from the latter, whom he promoted above himself, and he never addressed the people in the mosque until after Aḥmad's death. He would say, 'We have lost the sciences of realities with the death of Aḥmad al-Zaiyāt'. Al-Junaid also said, 'Abū Bakr al-Kisā'ī[65] asked me concerning a thousand questions which I would have hoped never to fall into the hands of the public'. This Abū Bakr was one of the greatest shaikhs; it was he concerning whom al-Junaid said, 'No one has crossed the bridge of al-Nahrawān to visit us who can compare with Abū Bakr al-Kisā'ī'.

Now I will mention a selection of those who have discoursed on these sciences, so that it may be known that no age has been without them.

Of those who have spoken to the people publicly is the Imam of Imams, Abū Sa'īd al-Ḥasan b. Abi 'l-Ḥasan al-Baṣrī.[66] He was accused during his time of subscribing to the doctrine of predestination, but he was a man of far too great account to have such suspicions harboured against him. How truly the poet observes:

'Complaint of a Stranger Exiled from Home'

Taghlib of Wā'il has no hurt
Whether you spread about them dirt,
Or urinate in just the place
Where the two seas meet face to face.[67]

Abū Nu'aim al-Iṣfahānī[68] wrote a book which he called 'A Defence of al-Hasan b. Abi 'l-Ḥasan against the ascription of predestination'. When 'Alī b. Abī Ṭālib (peace be upon him) saw al-Ḥasan al-Baṣrī he admired him and praised him; he gave him permission to discourse, and prohibited all who were preaching to the public in Basra to continue so, saying, 'This is an innovation; we never encountered it in the first age'.

Al-Ḥasan's discourse was comparable with the discourse of the prophets, and his rectitude with that of the Companions. Whenever Anas b. Mālik was questioned about any matter he would say, 'Ask our master al-Ḥasan'. Most of his discourse touched upon defects of actions, whisperings of the breasts, hidden qualities, and lusts of the carnal soul. He was once asked, 'O Abū Sa'īd, we observe that your discourse is such as is not heard from anyone else. Whence have you derived it?' He replied, 'From Ḥudhaifa b. al-Yamān'.[69]

Now Ḥudhaifa discoursed in a manner not heard from any other Companion. On being questioned concerning this he said, 'People used to question God's Messenger (God bless him) concerning good, saying, "O Messenger of God, what shall a man receive who does such and such?" I used to question him concerning evil, saying, "What is it that corrupts such and such?" When God's Messenger (God bless him and his family) observed me asking questions about defects of actions, he singled me out for this science.' He used to be called 'The man with the secret'. He was unique among the Companions as possessing the science of 'hypocrisy'[70]—a science which comprises, according to our savants, seventy chapters, knowledge of the subtleties and profundities of which is reserved exclusively to those 'travellers' who are 'firmly rooted in knowledge'. 'Umar, 'Uthmān and the leading Companions used to question him concerning the general and particular temptations, and he would inform them of those matters.

The following are amongst the ancient preachers who discoursed publicly:

Abu 'l-Sawār Ḥassān b. Ḥuraith al-'Adawī.[71]

Ṭalq b. Ḥabīb,[72] of whom al-Sakhtiyānī[73] said, 'I never saw anyone more devout than Ṭalq'.

Farqad al-Sabakhī,[74] who contradicted al-Ḥasan one day when he heard him discoursing. He said, 'That is not what our jurisprudents say'. Al-Ḥasan[75] replied, 'May your mother be bereaved of you, Furaiqad![76] Have you ever seen a "jurisprudent" with your own eyes? The true jurisprudent is he who has learned from God Himself what He commands and prohibits.'

Abū 'Āṣim al-Mudhakkir, one of the ancient shaikhs of Syria.[77]

Ṣāliḥ al-Murrī.[78] Sufyān Il-Thaurī[79] attended one of his classes, and marvelling at his discourse, said, 'He is the warner of his people'.

'Abd al-'Azīz b. Salmān,[80] who during one of his classes prayed for a paralytic, and he departed to his family walking.

Al-Faḍl b. 'Īsā al-Raqāshī.[81]

Among the famous shaikhs is Abū 'Alī al-Ḥasan al-Masūḥī.[82] He used to discourse in the mosque of Medina; al-Junaid attended his classes and derived knowledge from him. He did not discourse, however, on the science of 'attainment', but only on the science of the 'path'.

Abū Sh'aib al-Murādī named al-Muqaffa'.[83] In one of his revelations he was given the choice between a number of things. Out of them all he chose tribulation; he lost his eyes, hands and feet.

'Complaint of a Stranger Exiled from Home'

Among the great Sufis is Muḥammad b. Ibrāhīm called Abū Ḥamza al-Baghdādī al-Bazzāz.[84] He had something to say on all the Sufi sciences. Aḥmad b. Ḥanbal[85] used to question him on various things; he would say, 'What do you say on such and such, O Sufi?' He was the first man to discourse on these sciences in Baghdad. He met with a great response at Tarsus; people flocked to him; then they heard him, in a state of intoxication, saying things such that they testified against him as an atheist and an incarnationist. They therefore expelled him from Tarsus. His beasts of burden were impounded, and publicly proclaimed as 'the atheist's beasts'. When he was driven out of the town, he began to chant:

Thou hast a place apart,
Well-guarded, in my heart;
All insults heaped on me
Are light, if borne for Thee.

Amongst them also is the celebrated landmark Abu 'l-Qāsim al-Junaid b. Muḥammad,[86] as well as Naṣr b. Rajā',[87] one of his contemporaries. Then there are Abū 'Abd Allāh al-Balkhī,[88] and Abu 'l-Ḥusain b. Sham'ūn,[89] who held forth to the people in the mosque of Baghdad.

Abu 'l-Ḥusain 'Amr b. 'Uthmān al-Miṣrī,[90] who composed many sermons on the science of Sufism.

Mūsā al-Ashajj,[91] who was the first to discourse in Basra on the sciences of trust-in-God, love, and yearning. The way of the people of Basra before him comprised self-denial, personal endeavour, keeping to earning one's living, and the maintenance of silence, until God opened up the sciences of gnosis at the hands of Mūsā al-Ashajj.

Among the shaikhs of Basra is Fahrān al-Raffā',[92] who discoursed publicly in Baghdad.

One of their great ones is Abū Ja'far al-Ṣaidalānī,[93] who discoursed publicly in Mecca.

Among their famous ones is Abu 'l-Ḥasan b. Sālim,[94] one of the associates of Sahl b. 'Abd Allāh al-Tustarī.[95] His followers are named after him, being called the Sālimīya.

Abū 'Alī al-Aswārī.[96]

Abū Bakr b. 'Abd al-'Azīz, a shaikh of Mecca.[97]

Abū Sa'īd al-Qalānisī al-Nīsābūrī.[98]

Yaḥyā b. Mu'ādh al-Rāzī,[99] the greatest preacher of his time.

Abū 'Uthmān Sa'īd b. 'Uthmān al-Wā'iẓ al-Rāzī.[100]

Abu 'l-Sarī Manṣūr b. 'Ammār al-Būshanjī.[101]

Abū Bakr al-Shāshī.[102]

Abū Sa'īd al-A'lam.[103]

Abū Bakr al-Dabīlī.[104]

Abu 'l-'Abbās Aḥmad b. Muḥammad al-Dīnawarī,[105] who had a graceful tongue in these sciences.

Abū 'Ubaid al-Ṭūsī.[106]

Abū 'Alī al-Thaqafī,[107] one of the great savants of Khorasan. His name was Muḥammad b. 'Abd al-Wahhāb, and it was he who said, 'If a man mastered all the sciences, and associated with every class of people, he would not have attained the rank of true man unless he had disciplined[8] himself under a shaikh'.

Also among their great ones are 'Alī al-Ṭaiyān al-Fasawī[10] and Yumn al-Fasawi,[109] as also their fellow-townsman Abū Isḥāq Ibrāhīm.[110]

These men discoursed before the general public. Others of them did not discourse before the general public, but confined their preaching to their disciples. Amongst these is 'Āmir b. 'Abd Allāh b. Qais,[111] who was praised by the Imam of Imams, al-Ḥasan al-Baṣrī.

Mālik b. Dīnār,[112] one of the greatest ascetics and preachers of spiritual realities.

Abu 'l-Sha'thā' Jābir b. Zaid,[113] of whom Ibn 'Abbās said, 'If the people of Basra had abided by the pronouncements of Jābir b. Zaid, they would have sufficed them'.

Abū 'Imrān al-Jūnī,[114] who discoursed on wisdom.

Abū Wāthila Iyās b. Mu'āwiya,[115] who said, 'The man who does not know his own vices is a fool'.

Abū Muṣāhir Riyāḥ al-Qaisī,[116] whose preaching was upon the highest stations of love, yearning and propinquity.

Al-Fuḍail b. 'Iyāḍ.[117]

'Alī b. al-Madanī.[118]

Aḥmad b. Wahb al-Zaiyāt.[119]

'Abd Allāh al-Sā'iḥ,[120]

'Alī b. 'Īsā.[121]

Abu 'l-Ḥasan Ṣumnūn b. Ḥamza.[122]

Abū Sa'īd al-Qurashī.[123]

Abu 'l-Ḥasan b. Ṣadīq.[124]

Zakarīyā' b. Muḥārib.[125]

Abu 'l-Ḥasan.[126]

Abū 'Alī al-Warrāq.[127]

Abū 'Alī b. Zīzā,[128] one of the great associates of al-Junaid.

Abu 'l-Qāsim al-Daqqāq,[129] who, like the last-named, discoursed on the sciences of stray thoughts.

Abū Muḥammad al-Murta'ish al-Khurāsānī,[130] who said, 'Whoever is not jealous for God, God will not be jealous for him'.

Abū 'Alī al-Sulamī.[131]

'Alī al-Ḥammāl,[132] who said, 'The spiritual truths of Sufism have departed, and only their conditions have remained. A people has come into the world who seeks after repose, and imagines that to be gnosis. "Surely we belong to God, and to Him we return." '

Abū Hāshim al-Zāhid.[134]

Ibrāhīm b. Fātik,[135] of whom al-Junaid thought highly.

Aḥmad b. 'Aṭā' al-Rūdhabārī.[136]

Abu 'l-Faiḍ Dhu 'l-Nūn al-Miṣrī.[137]

Abū Sulaimān al-'Absī, known as al-Dārānī, whose name was 'Abd al-Raḥmān b. Aḥmad.[138]

His brother Dāwud b. Aḥmad.[139]

Sahl b. 'Abd Allāh al-Tustarī.[140]

Abū 'Abd Allāh b. Mānik, who has a well-known treatise.[141]

Abu 'l-Adhyān.[142]

Abu 'l-Laith al-Maghribī.[143]

Abū Sa'īd al-Funūnī, one of the great Sufis of Basra.[144]

Abū Ḥātim al-'Aṭṭār.[145]

Jamīl b. al-Ḥasan al-'Atakī.[146]

Abu Ja'far al-Wasāwisī, named Muḥammad b. Ismā'īl.[147]

Abū Bishr b. Manṣūr.[148]

'Uthmān b. Ṣakhr al-'Aqīlī.[149]

Abū Sa'īd al-'Uṣfurī.[150]

Sulaimān al-Ḥaffār.[151]

Abū Thu' āba al-Qurashī.[152]

Abū Ya'qūb al-Ubullī.[153]

'Abd Allāh b. 'Affān.[154]

Abū 'Abd Allāh al-Baṣrī.[155]

Muḥammad b. Abī 'Ā'isha.[156]

'Amr b. 'Uthmān al-Makkī.[157]

'Abd al-'Azīz al-Baḥrānī.[158]

Abu 'l-Ḥasan 'Ali b. Bābawaih.[159]

Abū Bakr al-Wāsiṭī.[160]

Al-Rabī' b. 'Abd al-Raḥmān,[161] who said, 'God has servants who in this world are full of grief, and who are looking eagerly to the world to come. The eyes of their hearts have penetrated into the celestial kingdom, and have seen therein God's certain reward; they have therefore redoubled their efforts and endeavours, when the eyes of their hearts beheld this vision. Those are they who have no repose in the present world, and whose joy shall come tomorrow.'

Abū 'Abd Allāh al-Sindī,[162] a companion of Abū Yazīd.

Abū Bakr al-Zanjānī.[163]

Ibrāhīm b. Yaḥyā al-Tibrīzī.[164]

Abu 'l-'Abbās al-Sammān.[165]

Ḥātim al-Aṣamm.[166]

Abū Yazīd al-Bisṭāmī.[167]

Abū Aḥmad al-Ghazzāl al-Nīsābūrī.[168]

Ja'far al-Nasawī.[169]

Abu 'l-Ḥusain Aḥmad b. Muḥammad al-Khuwārizmī.[170]

'Abd Allāh b. Muḥammad b. Manāzil.[171]

Abū Naṣr Fatḥ al-Naddī.[172]

Abū Bakr al-Ṭamastānī.[173]

Abu 'l-Ḥusain b. Hind al-Fasawī.[174]

Abū Isḥāq Ibrāhīm al-Dabbāgh.[175]

Al-Ḥasan b. Ḥamawaih.[176]

Abū Bakr Muḥammad b. al-Jūrī.[177]

Abū 'Abd Allāh Muḥammad b. Ibrāhīm al-Khushū'ī.[178]

Abū 'Abd Allāh al-Najjār,[179] and Ibn Baṭṭa,[180] both associates of 'Alī b. Sahl.[181]

Aḥmad b. Shu'aib.[182]

'Ubaid, nicknamed Al-Majnūn.[183]

All the foregoing discoursed on these sciences, and all of them perished before A.H. 300, though it is said that some of them were after that date.

A number of women also discoursed before men and women.

Such a one was Rābi'a al-'Adawīya,[184] to whom leading men amongst the ancients gave ear, like Sufyān al-Thaurī.[185] That right was conceded to her. It was she who said to Sufyān, 'You would be an excellent man, but that you love this world'. 'Abd al-Wāḥid b. Zaid[186] sought her hand in marriage, with all his high position. She refused to see him for several days, until his sisters interceded with her on his behalf. When he entered her presence, she said to him, 'O lustful man, seek a lustful woman like yourself'.

Another of them was Sha'wāna al-Ubullīya.[187] She discoursed to the devotees. Her fear of God reached such extremes that she was powerless to worship. Then she saw a dream by which the burden was removed from her, and she resumed her religious exercises.

Baḥrīya al-Mauṣilīya,[188] who wept until she went blind.

'Unaida,[189] grandmother of Abu 'l-Khair al-Tīnātī[190] al-Aqṭa', who had five hundred pupils, men and women.

'Ā'isha al-Nīsābūrīya,[191] the wife of Aḥmad b. al-Sarī,[192] who discoursed to women in Nishapur. She trained under Abū 'Uthmān.[193]

Fāṭima bint Abī Bakr al-Kattānī,[194] who died in the presence of Sumnūn[195] while he was discoursing on love. Three men died with her.

The following are amongst the famous authors on these sciences, and their ancient practitioners:

Al-Ḥārith b. Asad al-Muḥāsibī.[196]

Abū Isḥāq b. Aḥmad al-Khawwāṣ.[197]

Abu 'l-Qāsim al-Junaid,[198] the head of the sect and their most reliable authority.

'Alī b. Ibrāhīm al-Shaqīqī.[199]

Sakht al-'Askarī.[200]

Abū 'Abd Allāh Muḥammad b. 'Alī al-Tirmidhī,[201] who declared, 'I never composed anything deliberately; I consoled myself with my compositions when I felt depressed'.

Abū Bakr Muḥammad b. 'Umar al-Warrāq al-Tirmidhī.[202]

Abū Ja'far al-Nīsābūrī, named Aḥmad b. Ḥamdān b. 'Alī b. Sinān,[203] with whom al-Junaid corresponded.

Aḥmad b. Muḥammad al-Farkhakī.[204]

Abū 'Abd Allāh Muḥammad b. Yūsuf al-Bannā' al-Iṣfahānī.[205]

Abū 'Abd Allāh Muḥammad b. Khafīf.[206]

Abū Naṣr al-Sarrāj al-Ṭūsī.[207]

Abū Ṭālib al-Makkī,[208] whose discourse on these sciences is, as far as I have seen and as I think, without precedent.

This is a subject on which one could speak at length; but now I will return to the point which I was making. Just as every group of scholars employs technical terms, to understand the meaning of which one must refer to them, so in the same way when one hears the technical terms used by the Sufis, reference should be made to them in order to elucidate their true significance. Such terms are *baqā'* (continuance), *fanā'* (passing away), *'adam* (not-being), *talāshī* (annihilation), *qabḍ* (contraction), *basṭ* (expansion), *sukr* (intoxication), *ṣaḥw* (sobriety), *ithbāt* (affirmation), *maḥw* (effacement), *ḥuḍūr* (presence), *ghaiba* (absence), *'ilm* (knowledge), *ma'rifa* (gnosis), *wajd* (ecstasy), *kashf* (revelation), *maqām* (station), *ḥāl* (state), *firāq* (separation), *wiṣāl* (union), *isqāṭ* (rejection), *ittiṣāl* (conjunction), *jam'* (concentration), *tafriqa* (parting), *dhauq* (intuition), *fahm* (understanding), *wuṣūl* (attainment), *sulūk* (path), *shauq* (yearning), *uns* (intimacy), *qurb* (propinquity), *tajallī* (revelation), *ru'ya* (vision), *mushāhada* (contemplation), and such expressions as 'So-and-so continued *bi-lā huwa*'[209] (without personal identity), and 'He sloughed off his skin'.[210]

When the intelligent and impartial person hears such expressions, he ought to refer for their meaning to the one using them, saying, 'What did you mean by these words?' To pass judgement against the speaker, before seeking from him an explanation of what was intended by these expressions, and to condemn him as an atheist and a heretic, is truly a shot in the dark.

A certain Sufi wrote to one of the Imams some verses in which he asked him about the meanings of various Sufi technical terms. One verse only of these lines seems to me apposite to this summary:

What does one mean by 'He without He'?
What signifies 'Me, and not me'?

My purpose in all this is as follows. In the treatise which I composed in my youth, and which my enemies out of envy took as a stalking-horse whereby they contrived to injure me, I mentioned a number of Sufi expressions, such as, 'The power of everlasting Majesty shone forth; the Pen remained, the writer passed away'. 'The eternal He-ness covered me, and overwhelmed my transient he-ness.' 'The bird flew off to its nest.' 'If a single atom of what passed between the two of them became manifest, Throne and Chair would be annihilated.' These and similar words my adversaries have criticized severely, alleging that to be unbelief, atheism, and pretension to prophethood.

I will now mention a few anecdotes of the shaikhs, and the phrases used by them, as a proof that the Sufi employ these terms among themselves; for they are in common use with them, without any blame being attached to them; their books are stuffed with them.

Thus, al-Wāsiṭī said, 'Almighty God displayed what He has displayed of His handiwork as a proof of His Lordship. Then He annulled what He had manifested, for "All things perish, except His Face".[212] Creation, in comparison with His grandeur, is as a particle of dust without moment. Creatures have no way unto Him, save inasmuch as He has made for them the way of knowledge, whereby they have affirmed His being as they have understood Him.'

The sense of these words is exactly the same as what I conveyed in a section of the aforesaid treatise. I wrote, 'The truth is that God is the Multiple and the All, and that what is beside Him is the single and the part'. The meaning is that all existing things, in relation to the grandeur of His Essence, are as the part to the whole, the single to the multiple; since all existing things are but a drop from the ocean of His omnipotence. I did not mean by that that God was multiple in His parts—high exalted is God indeed above being open to division.

Close in meaning to this is their saying, 'Gabriel, the Throne, the Chair, and the celestial kingdom with them, all of these are as a grain of sand in comparison with what transcends the kingdom, nay, they are less than that'. The intention of this statement is not that God is greater than the world by virtue of the multiplicity of parts, but rather in the grandeur of His essence. The purpose was to refute the tenet of the philosophers, that God only created one thing.[213]

How indeed should this objection be valid, seeing that I mentioned in many places in the same treatise that duality cannot possibly be conceived of in regard to the Eternal One?

Similarly they have imagined, in certain of the phrases I used, a pretension to that real vision of God which Moses (upon whom be peace) sought, and was told, 'Thou shalt not see me'.[214] They have overlooked the clear pronouncement, not admitting of any interpretation, that 'it is unimaginable that anyone should see God in this world, neither saint nor prophet, with the exception of Muḥammad (God bless him and grant him peace)'.[215]

Regarding the Spirit I have mentioned statements exactly corresponding to those of the shaikhs from the standpoint of meaning, even if they be not exactly identical in words. The Sufis have indeed discoursed much on the Spirit. Thus, al-Wāsiṭī said, 'God manifested the Spirit out of His majesty and His beauty, and had it not been veiled, every infidel would have prostrated himself before it. Then, when the lights of the intelligences and the understandings emerged, they were annihilated in the lights of the Spirit as the lights of the stars and the moon are annihilated in the light of the sun.' From these words it can be established that by 'annihilation' they do not mean the non-existence of a thing in its essence, but rather its disappearance in relation to its observer.

Abū Sa'īd al-Kharrāz[216] said, 'God has drawn the spirits of His friends unto Him, and has delighted them with the recollection of Him'. This corresponds with my statement in that treatise, 'The bird flew off to its nest'.

Abu 'l-Ṭaiyib al-Sāmarrī[217] said, 'Gnosis is the rising of the Truth upon the secret hearts through the uninterrupted succession of the lights'. Al-Wāsiṭī said, 'When the Truth manifests Itself to the secret hearts, It does not leave in them any place over for hope or fear'. This is what I meant when I said, 'The everlasting He-ness covered him'.

Al-Junaid said, 'When the Sufi's breath blows from his heart, it does not touch anything without it burns it up, even the Throne'. The burning-up of the Throne is tantamount to its annihilation; and whoever vanishes from himself, is united with his Lord, and all else is burnt up so far as he is concerned. Thus, it is related in an anecdote of Abū Sa'īd al-Kharrāz that he said, 'I wandered in the wilderness, and suddenly a voice from the unseen said to me:

> *If of the world of being thou hadst truly been,*
> *Not by God's Throne and Footstall, nor aught,*
> *hadst thou been seen?*'[218]

Whosoever fears God in his private communions, is thereby brought to this state. Abū Muḥammad al-Jurairī[219] said, 'By purity of servitude freedom is attained, and by freedom, revelation and vision are attained'. By this 'vision' is not meant what Moses sought from his Lord, but rather another thing whose reality is manifest to those who possess it. To this al-Jurairī was also referring when he said, 'Whoever does not found his relations with God upon fear and vigilance, will never attain to revelation and contemplation'.

Abū Bakr al-Tiflīsī[220] said, 'Sufism is a state which neither heart nor reason can withstand'. Abu 'l-Ḥasan,[221] the master of Sumnūn,[222] said, 'Sufism is neither a state nor a time; rather it is a sign which destroys, flashes which consume'. Al-Khuldī[223] said, 'Sufism is a state in which the essence of Lordship is manifested, and the essence of servanthood is obliterated'. This was what I meant when I said, 'Knowledge, reason and heart were annihilated; only the writer remained, without himself'. Al-Murta'ish[224] said, 'Sufism is a state which a man guards jealously from both realms of being; he departs unto the Truth, and departs even out of his departing; the Great and Glorious Truth is, and he is not'. Abu 'l-Ḥasan al-Aswārī[225] said, 'Sufism is my forgetting myself, and my waking to my Lord'.

Dhu 'l-Nūn al-Miṣrī[226] said, 'God has servants who gaze with the eyes of their hearts upon the veiled things of the unseen. Their spirits wander in the kingdom of heaven, then return to them with the fairest gathering of the fruits of joy.' This is what I meant when I said, 'The bird flew off to its nest, and then returned to the cage'.

A man once worked himself into a state of ecstasy in a séance conducted by Yaḥyā b. Mu'ādh.[227] 'What is this?' someone asked. He replied, 'The attributes of humanity have vanished, and the laws of Lordhood have appeared'.

Abu 'l-Fawāris al-Kardī[228] was asked, 'What is unitarianism?' He answered, 'It is what is opened up to you from Him, not through yourself'.

Sulaimān b. 'Abd Allāh[229] said, 'Every breath containing the recollection of God is conjoined with the Throne'.

Abū Ḥāmid al-Iṣṭakhrī[230] related that he questioned Abū Ya'qūb al-Zābulī[231] concerning Sufism. He replied, 'It is that the essence of humanity is obliterated from you, together with the signs of whereness'.

Ḥabashī b. Dāwud[232] said, 'Sufism is the Will of the Truth in creation, without creation'.

Yaḥyā b. Mu'ādh said, 'Whoso sees along with the Beloved other than the Beloved has not seen the Beloved'.

Much of that treatise of mine turns around these principles. Every expression occurring in these anecdotes requires the preparation of rules and the laying down of fundamentals of the science of Sufism, so that its meaning may be fully realized. I do not propose to explain that now, for it demands that the heart should not be occupied and that the spirit should be free of care. But I am much beset in mind, and mightily bewildered by the trials wherewith fate has afflicted me—imprisonment, chains, and every manner of torment:

Misfortunes in so many ways
Cascade around me quite
As, were they poured upon the days,
They would be turned to night.

I composed that treatise fully expecting to win a good name whilst living, and after death, the prayers of all that read it that God should have mercy on my soul. Had it ever occurred to my mind that the consequences would be this that I have suffered and still suffer, I would never have embarked upon it.

I planted shoots, and hoped that they
Would fertile prove,
And that due season would display
Good fruits thereof.

If, when I look for harvest fair,
As was my aim,
The saplings bitter produce bear,
Not mine's the blame.

Now, since no reply has been offered to those accusations against me by any savant or Sufi—and they have an excuse which I fully accept, but cannot mention now, since it is both broad and long—I myself have taken up the pen, upon which I rely, and have answered the statement of my critic, excusing myself to him by means of this present treatise.

'Complaint of a Stranger Exiled from Home'

Whoever hopes, and may depend
On favours from a distant friend,
When life's misfortunes press me nigh
Upon my own hand I rely.

How then can one begin?—seeing that in the words spoken by the Sufis there are things which, if scrutinized by a biased critic, would provide him with a wide scope for objection. Thus, it is related of Ma'rūf al-Karkhī[233] that he said to a certain man, 'Pray to Almighty God that He may restore to me a particle of humanity'. Taken literally, these words are outrageous; the critic might well say that Ma'rūf had set himself up above Muḥammad the Chosen One (God bless him and his family). 'I am a man', the critic could add. 'I fly into a rage as other men do.' Now Ma'rūf had claimed that no trace of humanity remained in him. This statement is perfectly clear to those who have verified spiritual realities, but others do not comprehend it. It is the same with every science; it is understood only by those who have plunged deeply into it, and have dedicated their lives to exploring its truths and inner meanings.

The science of Sufism is the noblest and most obscure of all sciences; none but Sufis know its manifest and hidden meanings. I will cite a problem which can only be resolved in terms of the science of the Sufis, so that it may become clear to my prosecutor that he has no inkling of their sciences.

There is a sound Tradition of God's Messenger (God bless him and his family) that he declared on more than one occasion, regarding himself and certain Companions, such as Abū Bakr, 'Umar, 'Uthmān and 'Alī (God be well pleased with them), that they were of the people of Paradise. It is also recorded in the canonical books of Traditions that God's Messenger (God bless him and his family) said, in the course of a lengthy Tradition, 'Then I shall go in unto my Lord and, falling prostrate before him, I shall intercede for my community'. On the other hand it is stated in the two *Ṣaḥīḥ*[234] that he said from the pulpit, 'By Him in Whose hand the soul of Muḥammad is, I do not know whether I am of the people of Paradise or of the people of Hell.'

This is a real problem. Its solution is, however, obvious to those who have trodden the Sufi way, but not to those who do not understand the true meaning of ecstatic utterances.[235]

Abū Yazīd said, 'Almighty God looked down upon the world and said, "O Abū Yazīd, all of them are My servants, except you". So He excepted me from servanthood'. It is clear that if the critic should say, 'The Messenger of God (God bless him and grant him peace) used to say, "I am a servant," it is also mentioned of the other prophets that they said, "And appoint me of Thy mercy among Thy servants". How then is it admissible for one not a prophet to say, "He excepted me from servanthood"?'; that would be only natural. The problem only exists for those who have not trodden the Sufi way. For the Sufis, its solution is clearer than the sun. Even clearer than Abū Yazīd's words is the saying of al-Shiblī,[236] when he heard what Abū Yazīd had said: 'The Truth made revelation to me by means of less than that, saying, "All creatures are My servants except you, for you are I".'

To the same order belongs another saying of al-Shiblī; on being asked, 'Do you know of any joy in your soul?' he replied, 'Yes, when I do not find any commemorating God'. If the critic should say, 'This is unbelief, for all the prophets were sent to call men to God and to the remembrance of God. They only rejoiced when their call was answered; so how could al-Shiblī say, "My soul only rejoices when no one is recollecting God"? ' that too would only be natural.

Again, al-Shiblī used to say in his prayers, 'O God, make my enemies to dwell in the garden of Eden, and do not deprive me of Thee for so much as the twinkling of an eye'.

If the critic said, 'If God's Messenger (God bless him and grant him peace) used to say in his prayers, "O God, I ask Thee for Paradise, and I take refuge with Thee from Hell", how should it be admissible for any other to say what al-Shiblī said?', that also would only be natural.

It is similarly reported of more than one of the great Sufis that he said, 'Whoever worships God for a recompense, that man is vile'. Kulaib al-Sinjārī,[237] who was a man who knew affliction, said, 'If Job were alive today, I would do battle with him'. If the critic said, 'The man saying that challenged the prophets regarding their prophethood, and that is unbelief', from the literal standpoint he would be in the right.

More astonishing still is what is related of Shaqīq al-Balkhī.[238] He asked one of the shaikhs for a description of the gnostics. The shaikh said, 'They are those who, when they are given anything, render thanks, and when they are denied, endure with fortitude'. Shaqīq commented, 'This is a description of what our dogs are like in Balkh'. The shaikh thereupon asked him to describe the gnostics. Shaqīq said: 'When they are denied, they render thanks, and when they are given anything, they prefer others to enjoy it.' If anyone should say, 'God in His Book has more than once praised the people of fortitude and thankfulness, so how could Shaqīq equate them with dogs?' he would have a great effect on men's hearts, except indeed with those who know the doctrines of the Sufis and the habitual manner of their addresses.

When al-Wāsiṭī[239] entered Nishapur he said to the associates of Abū 'Uthmān,[240] 'What used your shaikh command you to do?' They replied, 'To be constant in obedience, and to watch for shortcomings therein'. Al-Wāsiṭī observed, 'He directed you to pure Magianism. Why did he not command you to be unmindful of obedience, being watchful only for its inceptor and maintainer?' If an adversary said, 'This is unbelief, since he claimed that the constant observance of acts of obedience was pure Magianism; and this is contrary to the words of Almighty God and of His Messenger (on whom be peace). For the Koran from beginning to end sings the praises of obedience and the obedient'—his statement from consideration of the literal aspect solely of the matter would be true.

Know, that the science of Sufism is divided into many branches, and that each branch is studied by its particular specialists. There are very few indeed who comprehend all the branches. Amongst all these branches is one called the science of the way, and this comprises many volumes. It was to one of these branches that al-Shiblī referred when he said, 'I wrote Traditions and Jurisprudence for thirty years, until the dawn broke and I came to every teacher under whom I wrote and said, "I desire the jurisprudence of God Almighty". Then not one of them spoke to me.'[241]

Among the things in that treatise over which they reprehended me is the proposition that Almighty God transcends all possibility of being comprehended by the prophets, much less by other men. By comprehension is meant that he who comprehends encompasses the perfection of the object comprehended. This is conceivable only of God. Therefore, none knows God other than God, as al-Junaid stated. The words of Almighty God, 'They measured not God with His true measure',[242] have been interpreted as meaning, 'They did not know Him as He should truly be known'. God's Messenger (God bless him) said, 'If you knew God as He should truly be known, at your prayer the mountains would move from their places, and you would walk on the seas. And if you feared God as He should truly be feared, you would know the knowledge with which ignorance does not exist. No one has attained that.' Someone said, 'Not even you, Messenger of God?' The Prophet replied, 'Not even I. God is too great for any to attain His state.'

Al-Ṣiddīq[243] (God be well-pleased with him) said, 'Glory be to Him Who has not appointed for creatures any way to know him, save by incapacity to know Him'. Aḥmad b. 'Aṭā'[244] said, 'There is no way for any one to know God, by reason of the impregnability of His impassivity and the absoluteness of His Lordship'.

Abu 'l-Ḥusain al-Nūrī[245] was asked, 'How is it that He is not attainable by reason, and cannot be known save by reason?' He replied, 'How should the limited attain the Unlimited?'

Abu 'l-'Abbās al-Dīnawarī[246] was asked, 'By what means did you know God?' He replied, 'By the fact that I do not know Him'.

Dhu 'l-Nūn said, 'He has not known God who has known Him, and he has not found Him who has penetrated His essence; neither has he hit upon the reality of God who has represented Him'.[247]

The foregoing presents a confusion only for one who supposes that knowledge of God's existence, and the existence of His Attributes—knowledge, power, life, will, speech, hearing, sight—is the same as the gnosis of God, and the comprehension of His Reality. That is not the case. The Sufis make a great distinction between the knowledge of God and the gnosis of God. Knowledge of the existence of the Eternal One is a simple matter; God Almighty refers to it with the words, 'Is there any doubt regarding God?'[248] But as for the comprehension of the reality of the Essence, and real gnosis, that belongs only to God. To that refer the words touching on this point, as I have mentioned above.

To know that there exists an eternal Artificer of this world presents no difficulty to the initiates of spiritual realities; on the contrary, to them it is clearer than the sun, and how could it be imagined that those possessed of eyes to see would dispute the existence of the sun? Of course, the blind have need of argument, so that such knowledge may accrue to them *via* their ears. How can it be conceived that doubt should be entertained regarding the existence of Him Who is the True Being, through Whom all else appears, and from Whom it is brought into being, but for Whom nothing that has being would exist in any way whatsoever? If indeed non-existence could be conceived of in relation to Him—high exalted is He above the possibility of non-existence—the existence of every thing would become void.

The gnostics do not regard God from things, rather they regard things in God. Thus Abū Bakr al-Ṣiddīq (may God be well-pleased with him) said, 'I never looked on anything but that I saw God before it'. This vision has nothing to do with the vision which will come in the next world. Vision is rather a term used in common by lawyers and Sufis for many meanings; however, it is no part of our present purpose to expatiate on that.

The Sufis have certain words which they call *shaṭḥ* (ecstatic utterance). This term comprises every strange expression that issues from its speaker in a state of spiritual intoxication, and in the violent upsurge of ecstasy. In such a state a man is unable to restrain himself, as has been said:

They gave me wine, and then they said
'Sing not'; but had they given instead
Sharauras's mountains such a wine,
Their anthem would have outsung mine.[249]

Similar to this is the saying of Abū Yazīd, 'I sloughed off my self as a snake sloughs off its skin. Then I looked, and behold, I was He.' He also said, 'O God, adorn me with Thy Singleness, and cloth me in Thy Selfhood, and raise me to Thy Oneness, so that when Thy creatures see me they will say, "We have seen Thee"; and Thou wilt be That, and I shall not be there'.[250]

'Complaint of a Stranger Exiled from Home'

There are many like sayings. This has also been expressed by them in verse. One of them said:

Between myself and Thee
An 'I am' fights with me;
Proclaim the loud 'Thou art'
And make 'I am' depart.[251]

The Prophet (God bless him) was referring to the like mystery when he said, 'My servant shall not cease to draw nigh unto Me by works of supererogation until I love him; and when I love him, I shall be his ear wherewith he hears, and his eye wherewith he sees, and his tongue wherewith he speaks'.[252] When the mystic is overwhelmed in such a state, and, robbed of his reason, he is annihilated in the radiance of the sovereign lights of eternity, if he should cry, 'Glory be to me. How great is my majesty!'[253] and the like as referred to above, he would not be taken to task; for the words of lovers should be concealed, not bandied about.

Thus it is related that a dove was being courted by her mate, and was repelling his advances. He told her, 'If you give in to me, well; if not, I shall turn the kingdom of Solomon upside down'. The wind carried his words to Solomon. He summoned the male dove, and asked him to explain himself. The bird replied, 'O prophet of God, the words of lovers should not be bandied about'. The answer pleased Solomon, on whom be peace.

Moreover, the expressions criticized are scattered through different chapters; if the passages preceding and following them were studied, it would be realized that there are no grounds for objecting to them. Besides, in the words of Almighty God and of His Messenger, expressions occur here and there regarding the Attributes of God the Great and Glorious which, if collected together and enunciated all at once (as the people in error have done), would give rise to great confusion, ambiguity and obscurity. If however each expression is mentioned in its appropriate place and along with its proper context, the ears would not reject them, neither would the instincts recoil from them.

In regard to Almighty God, expressions have occurred which are extremely ambiguous, and clearly susceptible of correct and mistaken interpretation. Examples of these are *istiwā'* (being seated), *nuzūl* (descending), *ghaḍab* (anger), *riḍā* (satisfaction), *maḥabba* (love), *shauq* (desire), *faraḥ* (joy), *daḥik* (laughter), *karāhiya* (dislike), *taraddud* (hesitation), *ṣūra* (form), *wajh* (face), *'ain* (eye), *yad* (hand), *uṣbu'* (finger), *sam'* (hearing) and *baṣar* (sight). Such too are God's statements:

> *Who is he that will lend God a good loan?*[254]

and

> *Do they not know that God is He who accepts repentance from His servants, and takes the freewill offerings?*[255]

Similar also are His words to Moses (upon whom be peace), 'I was sick, and you visited me not, hungry, and you fed me not'; so that Moses was agitated and sore troubled, and he said, 'My God, is it the case that Thou canst be sick and hungry?' God said, 'My servant so-and-so was sick, and my servant so-and-so was hungry. If you had fed the one and visited the other, you would have found me with them'.[256] This corresponds with what God revealed to David (on whom be peace) when he said, 'O Lord, where shall I seek Thee?' God replied, 'With those whose hearts are broken for My sake'.

Like to this also are Almighty God's words in the Book sent down upon our Prophet Muḥammad (God bless him): 'God is with those who are godfearing, and those who are good-doers';[257] 'God is with the truthful and the patient'; 'God is with the good-doers'. These are equivocal expressions on account of which many men have fallen into error, and others have turned atheists, saying, 'If prophethood were a reality, God's Messenger (God bless him) would never have described the Artificer of the world in terms implying corporeality, for corporeality implies contingency'. These men have been deluded by their own learning, and the lightness of their baggage in the sciences of the Arabic language. It is as the poet said:

How many a critic we have found
Belabouring a sentence sound,
The root of his misapprehension
Being his own sick comprehension!

The Koran refers to such men:

No; but they have cried lies to that whereof they comprehended not the knowledge.[258]

The Koran specifies them further:

And since they are not guided by it, certainly they will say, 'This is an old calumny!'[259]

Scholars rooted in their science are not ignorant of the true interpretation of these expressions. On the contrary, to them it is clearer than the sun; yet the majority of people have wandered astray concerning them, and have been bewildered as to their meaning.

Only the free-born man perceives
The darkling raincloud, and relieves;

Death's deepest agonies he sees
And, boldly battling, visits these.[260]

Had it been easy to reach the knowledge of the interpretation of these equivocal expressions, the Messenger of God (God bless him and his family) would not have particularized the Scholar of the community, 'Abd Allāh b. 'Abbās,[261] in his prayer, 'O God, instruct him in the faith and teach him the interpretation'. Yet despite the difficulty these expressions pose for the masses, to the elect they are easy to apprehend. The poet says:

I slumber with my eyelids tight
In their anomalies' despite,
Whilst other men the whole night through,
Sleepless, debate their meaning true.

If an atheist collected together these equivocal expressions that are scattered through the Koran and the Traditions, and consulted an Imam, saying, 'What do you say regarding a man who claims to be a prophet, and asserts that God knows hunger and sickness, anger and joy, that He laughs and loves and hates, and asks His creatures for a loan, and takes charity, and descends from on high to low, that His form is as the form of the sons of Adam, and that He has a face, hearing, sight, hands and fingers?' the Imam being consulted might well be unaware of the true purpose of the atheist, and that he was pursuing a secret aim quite other than his apparent object. He would therefore reply quite freely that whoever spoke such words had no knowledge of the reality of the Truth, and that his claim was false. This pronouncement would be based simply on the fact that the atheist had collected together expressions which ought to be kept apart, and that he had stripped them of contexts which ought always to be quoted whenever these words were mentioned, in order that they might not be ambiguous. Amongst the contexts which remove all possibility of error regarding these expressions are God's words, 'Like Him there is naught',[262] and 'Is He who creates as he who does not create?'[264]

If the mere collecting together of such expressions can have this effect, what is to be supposed if a substitution of terms is made, so that *movement* is substituted for *descending* and *repose* for *being seated*; if *palm* and *forearm* are mentioned in the place of *hand, ear* and *ear-hole* for *hearing, flesh* and *bone* for *face*, or *body* for *soul*? However, when the expressions *descending, being seated, hand, face,* and all the other ambiguous terms are mentioned exactly as they occur in the Koran and the Traditions, without change or substitution, combination or separation, augmentation or diminution, or being stripped of the words preceding and following them or denuded of their actual contexts, ambiguity will disappear from them, and uncertainty in regard to them will all but vanish.

How far from true learning is the man who cannot distinguish between the collecting together of these words on a single sheet of paper and mentioning them all at once, and their being cited along with other words which may exceed in all a million!

Why should I consider it so curious that the theologians of the present age should disapprove of me, seeing that the greatest scholars of every age have always been the object of envy, and have been the targets of every kind of persecution, men like Mālik, Abū Ḥanīfa, al-Shāfi'ī, Aḥmad and Sufyān,[264] God be pleased with them all? Victims of the same hostility have been the Sufi shaikhs such as al-Junaid, al-Shiblī, Abū Yazīd al-Bisṭāmī, Dhu 'l-Nūn al-Miṣrī, Sahl b. 'Abd Allāh al-Tustarī, Abu 'l-Ḥusain al-Nūrī and Samnūn the Lover. Works have actually been composed on such legal 'tests', and I would have mentioned some extracts from these, were it not that time will not allow of dwelling at length on this topic. So I have turned away from that, following the example of the poet:

From Nejd the shaft of lightning aimed,
And I exclaimed,
'O lightning, cares too burden me
To care for thee'.

It is no wonder that I am envied, seeing that I composed as a mere youth, sucking the udders of little more than twenty years, books which baffle men of fifty and sixty to understand, much less to compile and compose.

I do not blame them if they envy me;
Before my time,
And for no crime,
Savants have felt the lash of jealousy.

Any man wishing to check the accuracy of what I have stated, in all that I have remarked both already and hereafter, may seek out my works, examine their contents, and so scrutinize them as to master and fully to exhaust all the ideas expressed in them. The list includes my treatise called *Qirā 'l-'āshī ilā ma'rifat al-'ūrān wa'l-a'āshī* ('Entertainment of the night-traveller to recognize the one-eyed and the night-blind'), *al-Risālat al-'Alā'īya* and *al-Muftaladh min al-taṣrīf* ('Slice of syntax'), (the two latter being brief compositions), the treatise entitled *Amālī 'l-ishtiyāq fī layālī 'l-firāq* ('Dictations of yearning on the nights of separation'), the book named *Munyat al-ḥaisūb* ('The mathematician's desire') on Indian arithmetic, the treatise I named *Ghāyat al-baḥth 'an ma'nā 'l-ba'th* ('Goal of research on the meaning of mission'), another named *Ṣaulat al-bāzil al-anūn 'alā 'bn al-labūn* ('Assault of the sturdy nine-year-old upon the infant milksop'), and the book I entitled *Zubdat al-ḥaqā'iq* ('The cream of realities'). This was the last book I composed, being then twenty-four years of age. During this present year, in which destiny has put me to the test, I have reached my thirty-third year, the age of maturity which God the Great and Glorious has mentioned in His words, 'Until, when he is fully mature';[265] but a man does not attain complete equilibrium until he reaches forty.

Amongst the offspring of my thoughts are a thousand erotic verses which I was inspired to compose in ten days; these are collected together in a sheet known as *Nuzhat al-'ushshāq wa-nahzat al-mushtāq* ('The pleasure of lovers and opportunity of the passionate'). The following lines occur there:

Ah, and the maiden of Ma'add descent
On either side, the best of ancestry,
Guarded by warriors powerful as lions
Who raid the foe on noble, short-haired steeds,
Furnished with tempered swords of polished steel
And eke with slender lances, true and long!
She came, whilst my companions slept a-bed,
Escorted by her modest maids of Sa'd;
They trod the heights of hillocks and the vales
To visit a generous and mighty man;
Clad in the robes of glory and renown,
They passed the night in soft, delightful ease,
And I right cheerful, Hind being by my side,
Kissing her, mantled in sweet perfumery,
And culling with my lips the rose of her cheeks.

I had also embarked on the composition of two extensive books, each of which I intended to comprise ten volumes. The one, on the sciences of belles-lettres, I had entitled *al-Madkhal ilā 'l-'arabīya wa-riyāḍat 'ulūmihā 'l-adabīya*

('Introduction to the Arabic language and the practice of its literary sciences'); the other was on the interpretation of the real truths of the Koran.[266] But then religious concerns, and attention to my personal duties, prevented me from completing these two works. Whoever cares to discover my state of affairs, provided he is not impeded by ignorance, jealousy and a lack of impartiality, will know the truth of these claims which I am incapable of proving in the present circumstances, what with my distress, distraction, disorientation and mental dissipation. Let who so desires, therefore, turn his attention to verifying the facts.

Ask of Quḍā'a,[267] have I kept my trust,
Or did I fail my duty when in charge?
Many's the squadron's leader I have sunk
My lance in, many the fire of war I have braved,
Many the heroes whose like I have made them meet,
Poured them the cup of death, and drained it myself.
Many the brother who answered the call of the guest,
When the horses stumbled in the dust, I have lost.
So I shall seek out glory, neglecting naught—
If I die, then I die; if I live, I live.

And now it remains for me perforce to mention, in this brief essay, the true facts about the doctrine of the men of old, for there is a great need for such a restatement.[268] I will set them forth in three chapters, since the root principles of the faith are three—belief in God, in His Messenger, and in the Last Day. I shall treat each principle in a separate chapter, praising God and blessing Muḥammad the Chosen One and all the prophets. May God preserve us from error by His goodness and favour.

'Complaint of a Stranger Exiled from Home'

Notes

1. Cited in al-Subkī, *Ṭabaqāt al-Shāfi'īya al-kubrā* (Cairo, 1324/1906), IV 237.
2. See al-Jāḥiẓ, *al-Ḥanīn ilā 'l-auṭān* (Cairo 1333/1915), 29.
3. A mountain overlooking Hamadhan, mentioned often by the poets. See Yāqūt, *Mu'jam al-buldān* (Cairo, 1323/1906), I 208–10.
4. Mohammed ben Abd al-Jalil translates *al-ḥijāl* as 'aux anneaux d'argent'; but see Lane I 520.
5. Attributed to 'Ain al-Quḍāt, 'in a letter written whilst in prison to the people of Hamadhan', by Yāqūt, *loc. cit.*
6. A well-known ancient poet; for references see Abd al-Jalil, 196, fn. 2.
7. Ḥabīb = Abū Tammām the famous poet (d. 231/845 or 232/846), see *E.I.*[2] I 153–5.
8. See Abū Tammām, *Dīwān* (ed. Muḥammad Jamāl), 226.
9. The famous Bashshār b. al-Burd (d. 167/783), see *E.I.*[2] 1080–2.
10. Dhu 'l-Qurūḥ = the eminent pre-Islamic poet Imra' al-Qais, for whom see (*inter alia*) my *Seven Odes*, 31–66. The verses cited are quoted frequently.
11. Ibn Ḥujr = Imra' al-Qais.
12. A pre-Islamic poet whose extant works have been edited by W. Wright (1859) and translated by O. Rescher (1925); see Brockelmann I 21, Suppl. I 939.
13. A district in a valley on the slopes of Mt. Arwand. See Yāqūt, VII 273.
14. Cited in Yāqūt, *loc. cit.*
15. Quoting Koran 33 10.
16. Cited in Yāqūt, I 208.
17. These verses are frequently cited; see Abd al-Jalil, 200, fn. 2.
18. The Prophet's negro muezzin; his verses are frequently cited. Cf. Yāqūt, V 222, VII 390.
19. The author means *belles lettres.*
20. *Dīwān*, 259.
21. See 'Ain al-Quḍāt, *Zubdat al-ḥaqā'iq* (ed. A. Osseiran), 31, and cf. Abd al-Jalil, 205, fn. 3.

22. Cf. al-Sarrāj, *Kitāb al-Luma'* (Cairo, 1380/1960), 170.
23. Cf. Abū Ṭālib al-Makkī, *Qūt al-qulūb*, II, 23.
24. Cf. Koran 85: 16.
25. This instance of clairvoyance is cited frequently in Sufi books. See Abd al-Jalil 206, fn. 3; add al-Kalābādhī, *al-Ta'arruf* (Cairo, 1934), 44.
26. Anas b. Mālik, according to al-Qushairī, *al-Risāla* (Cairo, 1330/1912), 108.
27. This tradition is frequently quoted by the Sufis; add al-Kalābādhī, 8.
28. In 40/660, at the hand of Ibn Maljam the Khārijite; see *E.I.*[2] I 385.
29. For this incident see Hujwirī, *Kashf al-maḥjūb* (tr. R. A. Nicholson) (new ed., London, 1936), 84–5; al-Kalābādhī, 8.
30. Both editions read *kamālāt* ('perfections'), apparently in error for *kalimāt;* see Abd al-Jalil, 209, translating 'propositions'.
31. For this illustrious scholar, Algazel to the mediaeval schoolmen (450–505/1058–1111), see now W. M. Watt in *E.I.*[2] II 1038–41. 'Ain al-Quḍāt never met Abū Ḥāmid, but studied under his brother Aḥmad (d. 520/1126), see Introduction.
32. For details of these works, and their translations, see *E.I.*[2] II 1039–41.
33. For this verse see Abu 'l-Faraj, *Kitāb al-Aghānī* (Cairo, 1285/1868), XV 87.
34. See *Zubdat al-ḥaqā'iq*, 43 ff.
35. See *Tamhīdāt*, 30 ff.
36. For this famous pioneer of the 'intoxicated' school of Sufism, see H. Ritter in *E.I.*[2] I 162–3. He died in 261/874 or 264/877.
37. Not traced.
38. See Koran 24: 18.
39. Koran 12: 7.
40. Koran 12: 8.
41. Sufi author of *Qūt al-qulūb*, d. 386/996, see Sezgin I 666–7.
42. Koran 12: 7–20.
43. Koran 113.
44. *Al-talāshī*, a term rarely encountered in Sufi writings.

45. *Al-fanā'*, see *E.I.*[2] I 951.
46. See *al-Aghānī*, XV 92.
47. Not traced.
48. Attributed to al-Ṭā'ī in Ibn Qutaiba, *'Uyūn al-akhbār* (Cairo, 1928), II 8.
49. The Arabic originals of all these terms are set out alphabetically and explained in Abd al-Jalil, 286–97.
50. Koran 29: 69.
51. For the term *mujāhada* see e.g. Hujwīrī (tr. Nicholson), 195 ff.
52. Better known as a vegetarian, see L. Massignon, *Essai*, 43, 93, 148.
53. Died 227/841; see my *Muslim Saints and Mystics*, 80–6.
54. Uncle of al-Junaid, d. 253/867; see *ibid.*, 166–72. (Abd al-Jalil, 219, spells his name incorrectly.)
55. Koran 8: 29.
56. Founder of Koranic exegesis, d. 68/688; see *E.I.*[2] I 40–1.
57. Koran 24: 53.
58. Koran 7: 94.
59. Koran 2: 272.
60. Psalms III: 10.
61. For al-Junaid, head of the 'sober' school of Baghdad (d. 298/910), see *E.I.*[2] II 600.
62. See al-Sarrāj, *Kitāb al-Luma'* (Cairo, 1380/1960), 179.
63. See Abū Ṭālib al-Makkī, *Qūt al-qulūb*, I 159.
64. Died *c.* 270/883–4, see al-Khaṭīb, *Ta'rīkh Baghdād*, V 190.
65. Not traced.
66. For this famous early ascetic and preacher (d. 110/728), see my *Muslim Saints and Mystics*, 19–25.
67. Verse of al-Farazdaq, see Ibn Qutaiba, *al-Shi'r wa'l-shu'arā'*, 119.
68. Famous author (336–430/948–1038), see *E.I.*[2] I 142–3.
69. Died 36/656, see Ibn Ḥajar, *Tahdhīb al-Tahdhīb*, II 219–20; Ibn al-'Imād, *Shadharāt al-dhahab*, I 44. 'Ain al-Quḍāt's source was Abū Ṭālib al-Makkī, *Qūt al-qulūb*, I 150.
70. *Nifāq;* see al-Sarrāj, *op. cit.*, 456.
71. See Ibn Ḥajar, *op. cit.*, XII 123.
72. Died between 90/709 and 100/719. See Ibn Ḥajar, IV 31–2.

73. Died 131/748, see Ibn al-ʿImād, I 181.
74. Died 131/749, an unreliable transmitter of Traditions; see e.g. Ibn Ḥajar, *op. cit.*, VIII 262–4.
75. *Sc.* al-Ḥasan al-Baṣrī.
76. Diminutive of Farqad.
77. Not traced.
78. Famous ascetic, d. 172/788; see Ibn al-ʿImād, I 281.
79. Died 161/778, see *Muslim Saints and Mystics*, 129–32.
80. Not traced.
81. See Massignon, *Essai* 145.
82. Pupil of Bishr b. al-Ḥārith; see al-Khaṭīb, *op. cit.*, VII 366–7; al-Sulamī, *Ṭabaqāt al-Ṣūfīya* (Cairo, 1372/1953), 43.
83. See Jāmī, *Nafaḥāt al-uns* (Teheran, 1337/1958), 77.
84. Died 289/902 or 269/883; see al-Khaṭīb, I 390–4; al-Sulamī, *op. cit.*, 295–8.
85. Founder of the Ḥanbalī school of jurisprudence, d. 241/855; see *E.I.*[2] I 272–7.
86. See note 61.
87. Not traced.
88. Not traced.
89. Or Ibn Samʿūn, d. 387/997; see al-Khaṭīb, I 274–7; Ibn Khallikān, *Wafayāt al-aʿyān* (Cairo, 1367/1948). III 431–2; al-Yāfiʿī, *Mirʾāt al-jinān*, II 432–5.
90. Not traced.
91. Not traced.
92. Not traced.
93. Not traced.
94. Founder of the Sālimīja school, d. 297/909; see *E.I.*[1] IV 115.
95. Died 283/896; see *Muslim Saints and Mystics*, 153–60.
96. Not traced.
97. Not traced.
98. Not traced.
99. Died 258/871; see *Muslim Saints and Mystics*, 179–82.
100. Not traced.
101. See al-Sulamī, 130–6.
102. Not traced.

103. Not traced.
104. Not traced.
105. Died after 340/951; see al-Sulamī, 475–8.
106. Not traced.
107. Died 328/940; see al-Sulamī, 361–5.
108. Not traced.
109. Not traced.
110. Not traced.
111. Not traced.
112. Famous early ascetic, d. *c.* 130/748; see *Muslim Saints and Mystics*, 26–31.
113. Famous traditionist, d. *c.* 100/718; see *E.I.*[2] II 359.
114. Early traditionist, d. 128/746; see Ibn Ḥajar, VI 389.
115. Early traditionist, d. 122/740; see Ibn Ḥajar, I 390–1.
116. Not traced.
117. Famous ex-brigand, d. 187/803; see *E.I.*[2] II 936.
118. Not traced.
119. Not traced.
120. Not traced.
121. Not traced.
122. Died *c.* 300/915; see al-Sulamī, 195–9; *Muslim Saints and Mystics*, 239–42.
123. Not traced.
124. Not traced. Teheran ed. reads b. Ḥudaiq.
125. Not traced.
126. Not traced.
127. Not traced.
128. Not traced. Paris ed. reads b. Zīrā.
129. Not traced. Abd al-Jalil identifies with the teacher of al-Qushairī, but his *kunya* was Abū 'Alī.
130. Died 328/940; see al-Qushairī, *al-Risāla*, 26.
131. Not traced.
132. Not traced.
133. Koran 2: 151.
134. Not traced.
135. See al-Sulamī, 168; Jāmī, *op. cit.*, 152–4.
136. Died 369/980; see al-Sulamī, 497–500.
137. Very famous Egyptian mystic, d. 246/861; see *E.I.*[2] II 242.

138. Died 205/820; or 215/830; also called al-Dārā'ī (as in Teheran ed.); see al-Qushairī, 15; Ibn al-'Imād, II 13; al-Sulamī, 75–82.
139. Not traced.
140. See note 95.
141. See Jāmī, 266.
142. Not traced. The Teheran ed. spells Adyān.
143. Not traced. The Paris ed. spells al-Maghzī.
144. Not traced.
145. Not traced.
146. Pupil of Ibn 'Uyaina, see Ibn Ḥajar, II 113–14.
147. Not traced.
148. Not traced.
149. Not traced.
150. Not traced.
151. Not traced.
152. Not traced.
153. Not traced.
154. Not traced.
155. Not traced.
156. Not traced.
157. Pupil of al-Junaid, d. 291/904 or 297/910; see *Muslim Saints and Mystics*, 214–17.
158. Not traced.
159. Not traced.
160. Associate of al-Junaid, d. after 320/932; see al-Sulamī, 302–6.
161. Not traced.
162. Presumably for Abū 'Alī al-Sindī; see *E.I.*[2] I 162; Jāmī, 57.
163. Not traced.
164. Not traced.
165. Not traced.
166. Died 237/852; see *Muslim Saints and Mystics*, 150–2.
167. See note 36.
168. Not traced.
169. Not traced.
170. Not traced.
171. Died 332/944; see al-Sulamī, 123 fn. 2.

172. Not traced.
173. Died after 340/951; see al-Qushairī, 29.
174. Not traced.
175. Not traced.
176. Not traced.
177. Not traced.
178. Not traced.
179. Not traced.
180. Not traced.
181. Of Isfahan, a companion of al-Junaid; see al-Sulamī, 233–6.
182. Not traced.
183. Not traced.
184. Celebrated woman saint; see *Muslim Saints and Mystics*, 39–51.
185. Prominent lawyer and traditionist, d. 161/778; see *Muslim Saints and Mystics*, 129–32.
186. Leading ascetic, d. 177/793; see Ibn al-'Imād, I 287.
187. Frequented by al-Fuḍail b. 'Iyād; see Jāmī, 616; al-Sha'rānī, *al-Ṭabaqāt al-kubrā* (Cairo, 1343/1925), I 57.
188. Not traced. Abd al-Jalil misspells Buḥaira (234).
189. Not traced.
190. Died after 340/951; see al-Sulamī, 370–2.
191. Not traced.
192. Not traced.
193. Not traced.
194. Not traced. Her father died in 322/924; see al-Sulamī, 373–7.
195. See note 122.
196. Author of *al-Ri'āya* and other works, d. 243/857; see *Muslim Saints and Mystics*, 143–5.
197. Died 291/904; see *Muslim Saints and Mystics*, 272–6.
198. See note 61.
199. Not traced.
200. Not traced.
201. Famous author of *Khatm al-auliyā'* and many other works, d. after 318/930, see Sezgin, I 653–9.
202. Died *c.* 280/893; see al-Sulamī, 221–7.
203. Died 311/923; see al-Sulamī, 332–4.
204. Not traced.
205. Not traced.

206. Famous saint of Shiraz, d. 371/981; see Sezgin, I 663–4.
207. Author of *Kitāb al-Luma'*, d. 378/988; see Sezgin, I 666.
208. See note 41.
209. See Baqlī, *Sharḥ-i Shaṭḥīyāt* (Teheran-Paris, 1966), 615.
210. See Massignon, *Essai*, 246.
211. See note 160. For other sayings of al-Wāsiṭī criticized, see al-Sarrāj, 506–15.
212. Koran 28: 88. For the saying, 'God is the Multiple . . .', see *Zubdat al-ḥaqā'iq*, 21.
213. See e.g. al-Shahrastānī, *al-Milal wa'l-niḥal*, 380.
214. Moses in Sinai, Koran 7: 139.
215. On the occasion of his 'ascension' (*mi'rāj*), a matter of theological debate; see *E.I.*[1] III 507.
216. Important Sufi author, d. 279/892 or 286/899; see Sezgin, I 646.
217. Not traced.
218. See al-Qushairī, 34.
219. Died 311/923; see al-Sulamī, 259–64. The Teheran ed. wrongly spells al-Ḥarīrī.
220. Not traced.
221. Not identified.
222. See note 122.
223. Died 348/959; see Sezgin, I 661.
224. See note 130.
225. Not traced; *cf.* note 96.
226. See note 137.
227. Died 258/872; see Sezgin, I 644.
228. Teacher of Abū Yazīd al-Bisṭāmī; see Jāmī, 56.
229. Not traced.
230. Not traced.
231. Not traced. Abd al-Jalil emends to al-Mazābilī and refers to Massignon, *Ḥallāj*, 530.
232. Not traced.
233. Died 200/816; see Sezgin, I 637.
234. The canonical collections of al-Bukhārī (d. 256/870, see Sezgin, I 115–34) and Muslim (d. 261/875, see Sezgin, I 136–43).
235. *Shaṭḥīyāt*, for which see Massignon in *E.I.*[1] IV 335–6.

236. Famous ecstatic, d. 334/946; see Sezgin, I 660; *Muslim Saints and Mystics*, 277–86.
237. Not traced.
238. Died 194/810; see *Muslim Saints and Mystics*, 133–7.
239. See note 160.
240. Not identified.
241. See al-Sarrāj, 487.
242. Koran 6: 91.
243. Abū Bakr, the first caliph.
244. Died 309/922; see *Muslim Saints and Mystics*, 236–8.
245. Died 295/908; see *Muslim Saints and Mystics*, 221–30.
246. Died after 340/951; see al-Sulamī, 475–8.
247. *Sc.* likened Him to any created being.
248. Koran 14: 11.
249. See Yāqūt, v 258.
250. For a discussion of this famous saying, see my 'Bistamiana' in *B.S.O.A.S.*, xxv (1962), 28–37.
251. See Massignon. *Le Dîwân d'al-Ḥallâj*, 90.
252. For this famous saying, see my *Sufism*, 27, with note 11.
253. Famous *shaṭḥ* of Abū Yazīd al-Bisṭāmī; see *E.I.*[2] I 162.
254. Koran 2: 246; 57: 11.
255. Koran 9: 105.
256. Cf. St. Matthew xxv 35–40.
257. Koran 16: 128.
258. Koran 10: 40.
259. Koran 46: 10.
260. See Abū Tammām, *al-Ḥamāsa* (ed. Freytag), 21.
261. See note 56.
262. Koran 42: 9.
263. Koran 16: 17.
264. Mālik b. Anas (d. 179/795), founder of Mālikī jurisprudence; Abū Ḥanīfa (d. 150/767), founder of the Ḥanafīs; al-Shāfi'ī (d. 204/820), founder of the Shāfi'īs; Aḥmad b. Ḥanbal (d. 241/855), founder of the Ḥanbalīs; Sufyān al-Thaurī (d. 161/778), founder of the Thaurīs (extinct).
265. Koran 46: 14.
266. For 'Ain al-Quḍāt's surviving works, see the Introduction to the present book.

267. Quḍā'a, like Ma'add in the previous poem, was the name of a large group of tribes.
268. A similar purpose had animated al-Kalābādhī when writing his *al-Ta'arruf*; see the preface to my translation, *The Doctrine of the Sufis*.

CHAPTER ONE

Of Faith in God and His Attributes

Know that Almighty God is a being whose non-existence is inconceivable; One, whose division into parts is likewise inconceivable. He is the All-generous King, the Merciful, the Compassionate, the Majestic, the Splendid, Lord of the mighty Names. The hearts of all creatures are in His hand, and towards Him are turned the forelocks of all beings. No matter preoccupies Him from any other matter, and to His Majesty all authority submits. He has no partner in His unicity, no like in His singularity, no opposite in His impermeability, no rival in His oneness. His is the kingdom below and above, and all glory and grandeur are under His authority. He is the first of every thing, He was before every thing, and He shall endure after the passing away of every thing. He is the only praiseworthy, the glorious, and He accomplishes what He desires. He is sublime in His nearness and near in His sublimity, manifest in His latency and latent in His manifestation; and He is veiled from created beings by reason of the extreme luminosity of His light. He is the All-compeller, the Omnipotent, the Everlasting, the All-powerful; the last in His firstness, and the first in His lastness. He encompasses all things in His knowledge, and He embraces all the inhabitants of heaven and earth in His mercy and forbearance. His benefactions have been outpoured over both the terrestrial and the celestial kingdoms, and

With Him are the keys of the Unseen;
none knows them but He.[269]

His are the favours heaped one upon another, and the successive gifts, the overflowing grace and the comely generosity. To him belong the glory sublime, the marvellous works, the noble pardon, the eternal beneficence, the splendid openhandedness, the manifest kingship, the lofty splendour and the soaring sovereignty.

He created earth and heaven, and disposed the destinies therein in what manner He willed, measuring them and arranging them in the manner most fair. How many of His marvellous secrets inhabit every atom! His servants do evil to Him, and His goodness to them increases all the more; they court His hatred by acts of disobedience, and He will only be the more benevolent towards them. His bounties are infinite, His gifts innumerable. The eye cannot endure to gaze upon the perfection of His radiance, neither upon so much as its first manifestations. Every thing is submissive to His grandeur; the earths and the heavens are in His grasp and power.

Eternal is He, without beginning to His eternity; everlasting is He, without end to His everlastingness. He is permanent in being, without any passing away; perfect in essence through every circumstance. He is endowed with the attributes of perfection, described with the epithets of glory and beauty. He possesses the names most beautiful, the attributes most sublime. He does not resemble bodies, neither is He receptive to division. He is eternal in His essence, perpetual in His attributes. He was, before ever He created the earths and the heavens, and He is even now as He was, possessed of attributes complete and perfect qualities. He is not like to other beings whether in His essence or His attributes; indeed, all other beings are but a drop of the sea of His omnipotence, a sign of His signs.

Nought escapes from His eternal knowledge, not so much as the weight of an atom, such as a grain of dust; indeed, His knowledge of what is under His earth is as His knowledge of what is above heaven. All existing things are, in the expanse of His knowledge, as a drop in the oceans, a sand-grain in the deserts. No glance eludes his design, no thought His will. Whatsoever He wills, is; whatsoever He wills not, is not. Every accident that comes into being is produced in its foreknown time, as He designed it in pre-eternity and as He knew it before time began, without any addition or diminution, without advancement or postponement.

He is the All-hearing, the All-knowing; no thing heard escapes from His hearing, no thing seen eludes His sight. On the contrary, all the same with Him is he who speaks openly and he who conceals his words, all the same what the heart hides and what it reveals. The secrets of the consciences with Him are open to see. The understandings of creatures flag and fail to apprehend the perfection of His attributes.

He it is who speaks with the eternal speech, subsisting with His essence,[270] too sublime to resemble the speech of creatures. All that He has said, alike the clear and the ambiguous, is according to how He said it and designed it. His commands and prohibitions are true, His promises and threats are real. This we believe with a faith of verification and certainty; this we confirm as true with a sureness unadulterated by doubt.

Glorious is His face, and exalted His majesty, who is living unmenaced by death, abiding untouched by decay. He made manifest all existing things, by His omnipotence originating them; He reserved to Himself alone their creation as beings invented by Him. Glory to Him, Glory to Him! How great is His majesty, how manifest His proof, how perspicuous His sovereignty, how immense His goodness, how perfect His favour! The hearts fail to attain the means of describing His splendour and His magnificence. No man, however ambitious, aspires to comprehend His perfection, but that he is repulsed by the dazzling lights of His presence. How lofty He is in His glory, how brilliant in His beauty, how mighty in His grandeur, how manifest in the radiation of His light, how firm in His Lordship, how perpetual in His being, how sublime in His unicity, how glorious in His everlastingness, how eternal in His priority, how previous in His eternity! He is the inheritor of the inhabitants of His earth and heaven. He is the living, when naught living is, in the continuance of His kingship abiding for ever. Too mighty is He for any tongue to describe the perfection of His essence, or for any exposition to set forth in full the complete tally of His most lofty attributes.

Notes

269. Koran 6: 59.
270. A reference to the orthodox doctrine of the eternal and uncreated Koran.

CHAPTER TWO

Of Faith in Prophethood

Know that God Most Glorious sent the prophets as bearers of good tidings and as warners. He sent forth Muḥammad to the whole of mankind, Arabs and non-Arabs, black and red, and fortified him with evident miracles and shining signs. He abrogated by his law such of other laws as He willed, and confirmed of them such as He willed. He (Muḥammad) is the Seal of the Prophets and the Lord of men:

Far be it from time to bring his like to birth;
Time grudges to send his equal to earth.

Prophethood is a term denoting certain perfections which are given to prophets, and to attain which by means of reason is inconceivable. Reason has no other part but to confirm the truth of prophethood, and this it derives from consideration of the clear proofs and precise indications. As for a man attaining those perfections by means of reason, that is utterly impossible and preposterous.

The stage of prophethood is beyond the stage of sainthood. The final goal of the saints is but the beginning of the prophets. The stage of sainthood is beyond the stage of reason; the final goals of men of reason are the beginnings of the saints.

Whoever follows the doctrine of the philosophers and opines that 'prophet' is the term for a person who has reached the farthest degree of reason, and by means of reason has freedom absolute to issue commands and prohibitions, asserting that they are prescriptions which the prophet himself lays down and adjusts according to wisdom—

anyone believing this has disembarrassed himself of the yoke of Islam and joined the ranks of the idiots. On the contrary, he 'spoke not out of caprice', and his discourse was 'naught but a revelation revealed'.[271]

The true Imam, after God's Messenger (God bless him and give him peace), was Abū Bakr, then 'Umar, then 'Uthmān, then 'Alī (God be well pleased with them all). We know that by virtue of absolute unanimity resting firmly upon an unbroken chain of transmission.

In the flower of my youth I embellished an ode, sweeter than the heart's desire and more delicious than union with friends after a long separation, in which I praised God's Messenger (God bless him) and the right-guided caliphs (God be well pleased with them all); still more, I praised myself and my poetry in that I addressed myself to such a subject. The ode comprises seventy couplets, amongst them the following:

I shall spur on to him she-camels, emaciated
And jaded, exhausted by constant trot and gallop,
And I shall anoint the fevered eyelids and bleary
With healing dust in which his body is at rest;
And if my riding-beasts do not bring me to him,
May herbs never more rejoice them, nor waterhole
gather them.[272]

Notes

271. Koran 52: 3–4.
272. The theme is the pilgrimage to the Prophet's tomb. For the conventional allegory, see my *The Mystical Poems of Ibn al-Fāriḍ*, esp. 10–11.

CHAPTER THREE

Of Faith in the Next World

Know that the grave is the first of the stations of the next world; traditional accounts have come down to us regarding the inquisition of Munkar and Nakīr.[273] We do not give ourselves full rein on that by means of our feeble reason; for most of the circumstances of the next world are apprehended by the light of prophethood, and a few can be apprehended by individual saints and by single scholars deeply rooted in learning.

The grave is either one of the meadows of Paradise, or one of the pits of Hell. The fact that we do not see the pit or the meadow, neither Munkar or Nakīr, does not prove that the dead do not see them. For we are in the world of the lower, visible kingdom, whereas the dead are in the upper, invisible realm. The Prophet (God bless him and his family) declared: 'They are a pair of angels, churlish, harsh and blue; they scrape the earth with their fangs and trample on their hair. Their voices are like rumbling thunder, their eyes like blinding lightning.' Thereupon 'Umar b. al-Khaṭṭāb said, 'O Messenger of God, will this reason of mine be with me?' 'Yes', replied the Prophet. 'In that case', said 'Umar, 'I shall be equal to the test.'

Then 'that which is in the tombs shall be overthrown, and that which is in the breasts shall be brought out',[274] the souls will be restored to the bodies, and mankind will march forth unshod and naked. They will be mustered on the Resurrection plateau 'in scatterings', 'in a day whereof the measure is fifty thousand years'.[275]

Reason can only accept as true these possible things; as for apprehending them by its own means, that it cannot do.

Indeed, when reason apprehends the truthfulness of the prophets, and that it is inconceivable that lying can be alleged against them, then reason is compelled to accept as true all that the prophets have proclaimed, including the circumstances of the next world. All of that is real; such as the Balance, which will teach men the measure of their actions, the good and evil alike; and such as the Pathway, which is a bridge outstretched upon the back of Gehenna, sharp as a sword, fine as a hair; over it men will pass at various speeds, some like a bird in flight, some walking, some creeping along, some being hurled into Hell, 'into a place far away'.[276]

So too reason must assent to the reality of Paradise and Hell, along with the various sorts of pains in store in the latter, the severest being to dwell eternally in the Fire, veiled from God; also the different kinds of delights awaiting in the former, the highest being to gaze upon the Lord of All Being. Everything that has come down to us in the Koran, and has been spoken of in the sound Traditions, is real and true; we believe in it unquestioningly. Such likewise is the case with the Pool of which we shall come down to drink; whosoever drinks thereof but once shall not thirst thereafter for ever; sweeter than honey it shall be, whiter than milk.

Reason accepts the truth of intercession; first the prophets will intercede for us, then the saints, then the scholars, then the martyrs, and finally the whole mass of believers—every believer, as God's Messenger declared (God bless him), shall have the right of intercession.

This is the true creed which was agreed unanimously by the righteous fathers of the faith and the departed Imams. We have in them an excellent model and a well-approved example.

I have composed on the fundamental articles of faith some verses, as follows:

Of Faith in the Next World

I believe firmly, on proofs based upon reason,
That One Eternal exists (and this is no ignorant pretence),
Hearing, seeing, knowing, speaking,
Designing, omnipotent, living, bountiful.
Through Him subsists all that is in His highest heavens
And in His lowest earth, in rugged upland and plain.
We have no creator, no former and fashioner
Other than the One, the Everlasting, on high and below.
I have no doubt that He is the destroyer of men
And their lifegiver; He renews, and makes to decay;
And that God's Messenger is of His creatures the most excellent—
My word is 'a decisive word; it is no merriment'.[277]
I believe also that what Muḥammad delivered to us
Is as he spoke it, true, in branch and in root,
And that all that shall follow after death
Is as the Chosen One related, the Seal of the Messengers.
This is my creed, and the creed of my teachers,
And of my departed forebears, by Allah, before me.
Is there any Muslim, between earth's east and west,
Who gainsays this, rationalist or traditionalist?
How many in my cloak have been charged by their enemies
With foulness of speech and with infamous deeds!
I have no other occupation, by the Lord of the camels
Loping towards Minā,[278] *save this prayer to God:*
My God, cleanse the face of Thy earth of them;
And if what they say is true, cleanse it of the like of me!

It is better that I should restrict myself to this much, and not prolong my discourse, with all my present distress. I complain to God of these who have violated the rights of learning, and acted in a manner contrary to the accepted code of decent men. They have slandered me before the secular arm, and invented great falsehoods against me. Neither the theologians of the sects, nor the wearers of patched frocks and rags and tatters,[279] have performed their duty by me. They have delivered me over to my adversaries, to conciliate or declare war on as I choose. How worthy they are to have quoted regarding them the words of the poet:

What is this kinship that is not respected?
What is this blood-tie that's denied compassion?

God knows that I have never ceased to aid them in their quests, to procure their purposes, to bring them to their desires, to succour them with hand and tongue, to requite their evil with good, to bind up any of them that was broken, to free him that was in prison, to reform the corrupt, to repel from them the envious, to confirm their opinions, to fortify their hopes, to teach the ignorant amongst them what God had taught me, and to fill their ears with marvellous sayings and their hearts with delicate words of wisdom.

No other crime is mine but these—
The gems I loosed upon the breeze,
The necklaces I firmly strung
With wisdom for the old and young.

God shall be my judge, and theirs, 'the day when they shall not speak, neither be given leave, and excuse themselves'.[280]

Praise belongs to God, the Lord of all Being, for all His manifold benefits, and may His blessing rest upon Muḥammad and his immaculate descendants.

God is sufficient for us; an excellent
Guardian is He.[281]

Notes

273. The two angels who interrogate the newly dead; see *E.I.*[1] III 724–5.
274. Koran 100: 9–10.
275. Koran 7: 4.
276. Koran 22: 32.
277. Koran 86: 13–14.
278. On the pilgrimage; Minā is to the east of Mecca, see *E.I.*[1] III 498–9.
279. *Sc.* the Sufis.
280. Koran 77: 35–6.
281. Koran 3: 167.

APPENDIX

A

Brief reference has been made above (18, n. 15) to the problem set by 'Ain al-Quḍāt's statement that his youthful *Risāla*, quoted by his accusers, was composed twenty years earlier than his Apologia. Mohammed ben Abd al-Jalil suggested that this was a scribal error for 'ten', and raised the query whether the *Risāla* was to be identified with the then as yet unpublished *Zubdat al-ḥaqā'iq*. Now that this text is available in print, the problem of identification can be almost certainly solved in a positive manner.

In his Apologia our author cites a number of passages and phrases from the *Risāla* which had been fastened upon by his adversaries. Here below these quotations are itemized, identified (the pagination is that of the Teheran edition) in both original and translation, and then compared with their exact or near equivalents in the *Zubdat al-ḥaqā'iq* (Teheran edition).

(1) A 9. 8–9: *bal adda'ī anna ḥaqīqata 'l-nubuwwati 'ibāratun 'an ṭūrin warā'a ṭūri l-wilāyati wa-anna 'l-wilāyata 'ibāratun 'an ṭūrin warā'a ṭūri 'l-'aqli.*

Transl.: What I claim is rather that the inner nature of prophecy indicates a stage beyond the stage of sainthood, and that sainthood indicates a stage beyond the stage of reason.

Z 31. 1–2: *idh al-nubuwwatu 'ibāratun 'an ṭūrin warā'a 'l-'aqli wa-warā'a hādhā 'l-ṭūri 'lladhī sabaqat al-isharātu ilaihi* (*ya'nī al-wilāyata*).

(Transl.: Since prophecy indicates a stage beyond reason, and beyond this stage to which reference has been made previously (*i.e.* sainthood).)

(2) A 9, 15–16: *annahu yanbū'u 'l-wujūdi wa-maṣdaru 'l-wujūdi.*

Transl.: that He is 'the source and origin of being'.

Z 14, 15: *huwa maṣdaru 'l-wujūdi.*

(3) A 10, 13: *ḥājata 'l-murīdi ilā shaikhin.*

Transl.: the need of the neophyte for a spiritual instructor.

See Z 71–2.

(4) A 27, 2: *ashraqat salṭanatu 'l-jalālati 'l-azalīyati fa-baqiya 'l-qalamu wa-faniya 'l-kātibu.*

Transl.: 'The power of everlasting Majesty shone forth; the Pen remained, the writer passed away.'

Z 85, 10–11; *ashraqat salṭanatu 'l-jalālati 'l-azalīyati fa-talāshā 'l-'ilmu wa'l-'aqlu wa-baqiya 'l-kātibu bi-lā huwa.*

(Transl.: The power of everlasting Majesty shone forth; knowledge and reason were naughted, and the writer remained without individuality).

(5) A 27, 3: *ghashiyat-nī 'l-huwiyyatu 'l-qadīmatu fa'staghraqat huwiyyatī 'l-ḥadīthata.*

Transl.: 'The eternal He-ness covered me, and overwhelmed my transient he-ness.'

A 29, 1: *ghashiyat-hu 'l-huwiyyatu 'l-azalīyatu.*

Transl.: 'The everlasting He-ness covered him.'

Z 85, 11: *ghashiyat-hu 'l-huwiyyatu 'l-ḥaqīqiyyatu fa-'staghraqat huwiyyata-hu 'l-majāziyyata.*

(Transl.: The real He-ness covered him, and overwhelmed his phenomenal he-ness.)

(6) A 27, 3–4; 28, 16: *ṭāra 'l-ṭā'iru ilā 'ishshi-hi.*

Transl.: 'The bird flew off to its nest.'

Z 86, 5: *fa-ṭāra 'l-ṭā'iru ilā 'ishshi-hi.*

(7) A 27, 4: *lau ẓahara mimmā jarā baina-huma dharratun la-talāshā 'l-'arshu wa'l-kursiyyu.*

Transl.: 'If a single atom of what passed between the two of them became manifest, Throne and Chair would be annihilated.'

Z 86, 14–15: *lau ẓaharat mimmā jarā baina-huma dharratun fī 'ālami-kum hādhā la-talāshā 'l-'arshu wa'l-kursiyyu.*

(Transl.: add: 'in this world of yours'.)

(8) A 27, 13–14: *al-ḥaqqu anna 'llāha huwa 'l-kathīru wa'l-kullu wa-anna mā siwā-hu huwa 'l-wāḥidu wa'l-juz'u.*

Transl.: 'The truth is that God is the Multiple and the All, and that what is beside Him is the single and the part.'

Z 21, 13–14: *wa'l-ḥaqqu anna 'llāha (jalla wa-'alā) huwa 'l-kathīru wa'l-kullu wa-anna kulla mā 'adā-hu huwa 'l-wāḥidu wa'l-juz'u.*

(Transl. add: 'God (glorious and sublime is He) . . . and that all that is beside Him.')

A consideration of the closeness of these correspondences,

having regard to the probability that 'Ain al-Quḍāt was quoting from memory, and that in any case the text of the Apologia rests upon a very slender foundation, leads to the conclusion that the *Zubdat al-ḥaqā'iq* is indeed to be identified with his youthful *Risāla*.

APPENDIX

B

'Ain al-Quḍāt acknowledges, as we have seen, his prime indebtedness to the *Iḥyā' 'ulūm al-dīn* of Abū Ḥāmid al-Ghazālī (d. 505/1111); he also refers to the same author's *Mishkāt al-anwār* and *al-Munqidh min al-ḍalāl*. The only other Sufi book which he singles out for special praise is the *Qūt al-qulūb* of Abū Ṭālib al-Makkī (d. 386/996), from which he quotes verbatim, and which was one of the chief sources of the *Iḥyā'*. He names a minor work of the historian and biographer Abū Nu'aim al-Iṣfahānī (d. 430/1038), but seems not to be aware of his most important book on the saints and mystics, the *Ḥilyat al-auliyā'*. He gives us an extensive list of those who discoursed publicly on the Sufi sciences, not a few of them otherwise unknown, but is so faulty in his chronology that he states that 'all of them perished before AB 300, though it is said that some of them were after that date'.

When he comes to catalogue 'the famous authors in these sciences', we are struck equally by those included and those omitted. Of eminent personalities, he names al-Muḥāsibī (d. 243/857). al-Junaid (d. 298/910), Abū 'Abd Allāh al-Tirmidhī (d. after 318/930), Ibn Khafīf (d. 371/981), Abū Naṣr al-Sarrāj (d. 378/988) and Abū Ṭālib al-Makkī; he also includes in his list no fewer than four utterly obscure persons.

Far more remarkable is the long tally of Sufi authors considered today to be of the first rank, whom 'Ain al-Quḍāt totally ignores. It makes an impressive list, and seriously challenges his claim to authority:

Abū Sa'īd al-Kharrāz (d. 279/892 or 286/899).
Sahl al-Tustarī (d. 283/896).
Al-Ḥallāj (d. 309/922), but see below.
Al-Niffarī (d. 366/977).
Al-Dailamī (fl. 4/10th century).
Al-Kalābādhī (d. 380/990 or 384/994).
Al-Sulamī (d. 412/1021).

Al-Qushairī (d. 465/1072).

Al-Anṣārī (d. 481/1088).

Equally ignored is the famous Persian author Hujwīrī (d. *c.* 467/1070).

One can only conclude that the writings of these famous authors were not available to 'Ain al-Quḍāt, either in Hamadhan or Baghdad.

APPENDIX

C

'Ain al-Quḍāt put up a good defence against the charges brought against him, based, as we now see, upon phrases occurring in his *Zubdat al-ḥaqā'iq*. He was nevertheless condemned and executed. This was probably inevitable in the doctrinal and political circumstances. Yet his condemnation would have been even more peremptory, had his accusers been able to read Persian, and had they had access to his *Tamhīdāt*; for that book contains passages revolting in the extreme to strict orthodoxy, echoing ideas the publication of which had proved fatal to al-Ḥallāj.

Here are presented some passages from the *Tamhīdāt* which express a selection of 'Ain al-Quḍāt's more original and challenging ideas. The references are to the paragraphs into which the Persian editor has divided the text.

(169) People have heard the name of Iblis, but they do not know why he puts on such airs, and has no care for anyone. Why does he put on such airs? Because he came as a fellow-companion to cheek and mole. What say you? Do cheek and mole ever attain perfection without tress and eyebrow and hair? No, by Allah, they do not attain perfection. Do you not see that when praying it is necessary to say, 'I take refuge with God from Satan the stoned'? It is for this reason that airs and conceit and coquetry have filled his head, and he is himself the ring-leader of the arrogant and self-regarding. 'Thou createdst me of fire, and him Thou createdst of clay' (Koran 7: 12) is an expression of this same pride.

(170) If you do not believe this, then listen to God: 'Praise belongs to God who created the heavens and the earth and appointed the shadows and light' (Koran 6: 1). What perfection does blackness possess without whiteness, and whiteness without blackness? None. Divine wisdom so decreed; the All-Wise knew in His wisdom that so it must be and so it should be.

(171) My friend, give ear to what that great sage said regarding these two stages. He said 'Unbelief and faith are stations beyond

the Throne, veils between God and the servant'. This is because a man must be neither unbeliever nor Muslim.

(175) Do you know what this sun is? It is the Muhammadan Light which emerges from the eternal east. And do you know what moonshine is? It is the black light of Azrael which emerges from the everlasting west. 'Lord of the Two Easts and Lord of the Two Wests' (Koran 55: 16–17) expresses this exactly.

(245) Wisdom is this, that whatever is and was and may be, may not and might not be otherwise. Whiteness could never be without blackness. Heaven would not have been proper without earth. Substance could not be imagined without accident. Muḥammad could not have been without Iblis. Obedience could not exist without disobedience, neither unbelief without faith. Muḥammad's faith could not be without the unbelief of Iblis. If it were possible that 'He is God, the Creator, the Maker, the Shaper' (Koran 59: 24) did not exist, it would be possible that Muḥammad and the faith of Muḥammad might not exist; and if it could be that 'the All-mighty, the All-compeller, the All-sublime' (Koran 59: 23) did not exist, it could be that Iblis and his unbelief might not exist. So it is evident that Muḥammad's happiness would not exist without the misery of Iblis. . . . The Chosen One was the cause of the mercy shown to mortals, but in reality Abū Jahl was the cause of that.

(283) That mad lover whom you call Iblis in this world—do you not know by what name he is called in the Divine world? If you know his name, by calling him by that name you know yourself an unbeliever. Alas, what do you hear? This mad one loved God. Do you know what came as the touchstone of his love? One, affliction and oppression; two, reproach and humiliation. They said, 'You lay claim to love Us. There must be a token.' They offered him the touchstone of affliction and oppression, of reproach and humiliation. He accepted. Immediately these two touchstones bore witness that the token of love is truthfulness. Will you never understand what I am saying? In love there must be cruelty, and there must be fidelity, so that the lover may be ripened by the kindness and oppression of the Beloved; else, he will remain immature, and nothing will come from him.

(290) Friend, do you know whence his (Iblis') agony derives? His agony springs from the fact that at first he was the treasurer of Paradise, and one of the angels stationed near to God. From that station he came down to the station of this lower world, and was appointed treasurer of this world and of Hell. . . . Do you know what he said? He said, 'For so many thousands of years I attended diligently the street of the Beloved. When He accepted me, my portion from Him was rejection. When His mercy came upon me, He cursed me saying, "Upon thee shall rest My curse, till the Day of Doom" ' (Koran 38: 87).

(293) Just as Gabriel and Michael and the other angels heard in the Unseen, 'Bow yourselves to Adam' (Koran 7: 10), in the Unseen of the Unseen of the world unseen and visible He (God) also said (to Iblis), 'Do not bow yourself to other than Me' . . . So, openly He says to him, 'Bow yourselves to Adam', and secretly He said to him, 'Iblis, say, "Shall I bow myself unto one Thou hast created of clay?" ' (Koran 17: 63).

(393) 'Indwelling' will here display itself. Friend, if you desire to be granted eternal happiness, for one moment keep the company of an 'indweller' who is a Sufi, so that you may know what manner of being an 'indweller' is. Perchance it was of this that that shaikh spoke: 'The Sufi is God.'

(461) Here the saying of that great saint comes in. A disciple asked him, 'Who is your shaikh?' He said, 'God'. The disciple said, 'Who are you?' He answered, 'God'. The disciple asked, 'Whence do you come?' The shaikh replied, 'From God'.

For Product Safety Concerns and Information please contact our EU representative GPSR@taylorandfrancis.com
Taylor & Francis Verlag GmbH, Kaufingerstraße 24, 80331 München, Germany

www.ingramcontent.com/pod-product-compliance
Lightning Source LLC
Chambersburg PA
CBHW070545300426
44113CB00011B/1795
* 9 7 8 1 0 3 2 5 8 7 4 3 1 *